MORE
NEW TESTAMENT
WORDS

by the same author

MORE
NEW TESTAMENT
WORDS

WILLIAM BARCLAY

HARPER & BROTHERS   PUBLISHERS   NEW YORK

Library of Congress catalog card number: 58–10375

Silence is indeed the friend and help-
meet of thought and invention; but,
if one aims at readiness of speech and
beauty of discourse, he will get at
them by no other discipline than the
study of words, and their constant
practice.

GREGORY THAUMATURGUS
The Panegyric on Origen I

To

A.W.H. and E.H.

to whom I
and all who write and read
owe so great a debt

CONTENTS

7

ABBREVIATIONS

OT   Old Testament

NT   New Testament

AV   Authorized Version

ARSV   American Standard Revised Version

ibid.   in the same place

PREFACE

I T was to myself a very real surprise and a very great joy
when the publishers of *A New Testament Wordbook* in-
formed me that they believed that another volume on the
same lines was to be desired. This volume once again consists of articles which previously appeared in the pages of
the *British Weekly*, and once again I desire to express my
very sincere thanks to Mr Shaun Herron, the editor of that
paper, for the opportunity to write them in the first place,
and for permission now to republish them in more
permanent form.

The more I study words, the more I am convinced of
their basic and fundamental importance. On the meaning
of words everything depends No one can build up a
theology without a clear definition of the terms which are
to be used in it. No one can construct a Christian ethic
without a close study of the great ethical terms of the New
Testament. Christian belief and Christian action both
depend on a clear understanding of the meaning of words.
For such an understanding, although a dictionary is an
indispensable tool, much more than a dictionary is necessary. A word is like a person, in that it has a history and an
heredity. A word is like a person in that it keeps certain
company, and it is known by the company that it keeps.
No one would claim that all the history and the associations of a word are in the conscious mind of the person
who uses it, but it remains true that a word, by its history,
its pedigree, and its experience, acquires a certain atmosphere and flavour. It is the aim of this book to trace the
history and the usage and the associations of certain New
Testament words, that they may be better understood; and
that task is undertaken, not simply for linguistic reasons,

but that the writer himself, and those who read this book, may understand more of the meaning of the Christian faith and the demand of the Christian life. In this book certain of the words treated are examined at greater length and in greater detail than was commonly the case with the words in its predecessor. The reason for that is the greatness and the importance of the words so examined.

In the preface to *A New Testament Wordbook* I set out a fairly full bibliography, to which those interested are referred; but to that bibliography one invaluable addition must be made:

A Greek-English Lexicon of the New Testament and other Early Christian Literature, translated and edited by W. F. Arndt and F. W. Gingrich from the German *Griechisch-deutsches Wörterbuch zu den Schriften des Neuen Testaments u. der übrigen urchristlichen Literatur* (Preuschen-Bauer, fourth edition 1949-52): Cambridge University Press, 1957.

This volume is completely indispensable to the student of the language of the New Testament. It has, of course, always been available in German, but this beautifully produced English translation now makes it available to many who otherwise could not have used it.

I cannot end this foreword without expressing my most sincere thanks to the Editor and the staff of the SCM Press for the constant encouragement and help which they have given me.

This is the kind of book which anyone with a competent knowledge of classical Greek and of the Greek of the New Testament could well have written for himself. It is my hope and my prayer that it may do something to help those who never had the opportunity to learn Greek to understand the New Testament a little better.

Trinity College   WILLIAM BARCLAY
Glasgow
1957.

AGAPĒ AND AGAPAN

THE GREATEST OF THE VIRTUES

GREEK is one of the richest of all languages and it has an unrivalled power to express shades of meaning. It therefore often happens that Greek has a whole series of words to express different shades of meaning in one conception, while English has only one. In English we have only one word to express all kinds of *love*; Greek has no fewer than four. *Agapē* means *love*, and *agapan* is the verb which means to *love*. Love is the greatest of all the virtues, the characteristic virtue of the Christian faith. We shall therefore do well to seek to discover its meaning. We shall best begin by comparing these words with the other Greek words for love, so that we can discover their distinctive character and flavour. We begin, then, by looking at the other Greek words for love.

1. The noun *erōs* and the verb *eran* are mainly used for love between the sexes. They can be used for such things as the passion of ambition and the intensity of patriotism; but characteristically they are the words for physical love. Gregory Nazianzen defined *erōs* as 'the hot and unendurable desire'. Xenophon in the *Cyropædia* (5.1.11) has a passage which exactly shows the meaning of *erōs* and *eran*. Araspas and Cyrus are discussing the different kinds of love and Araspas says: 'A brother does not fall in love with his sister, but somebody else falls in love with her; neither does a father fall in love with his daughter, but somebody else does, for fear of God and the law of the land are sufficient to prevent such love' (*erōs*). The predominant connexion of these two words is with sexual love. In the English language the word *lover* can bear a lower sense;

11

and in Greek the meaning of these two words had degenerated so that they stood for lower things. Christianity could hardly have annexed these words for its own uses; and they do not appear in the NT at all.

2. The noun *storgē* and the verb *stergein* have specially to do with *family affection*. They can be used for the love of a people for their ruler, or for the love of a nation or household for their tutelary god; but their regular use is to describe the love of parents for children and children for parents. Plato writes: 'A child loves (*stergein*) and is loved by those who begat him' (*Laws* 754b). A kindred word occurs very often in wills. A legacy is left to a member of the family *kata philostorgian*, i.e. 'because of the *affection* that I have for you'. These words do not occur in the NT but a kindred adjective does once. The adjective *philostorgos* occurs in Paul's great ethical chapter, in Rom. 12.10, where the AV translates it *kindly-affectioned*. That is suggestive, because it implies that the Christian community is not a *society*, but a *family*.

3. The commonest words for *love* in Greek are the noun *philia* and the verb *philein*. There is a lovely warmth about these words. They mean to look on someone with affectionate regard. They can be used for the love of friendship and for the love of husband and of wife. *Philein* is best translated *to cherish*: it includes physical love, but it includes much else beside. It can sometimes even mean *to kiss*. These words have in them all the warmth of real affection and real love. In the NT *philein* is used of the love of father and mother and son and daughter (Matt. 10.37). It is used of the love of Jesus for Lazarus (John 11.3, 36); and once it is used of the love of Jesus for the beloved disciple (John 20.2). *Philia* and *philein* are beautiful words to express a beautiful relationship.

4. By far the commonest NT words for *love* are the noun *agapē* and the verb *agapan*. We shall deal, first, with the noun. *Agapē* is not a classical word at all; it is doubtful if there is any classical instance of it. In the Septuagint it is

used 14 times of sexual love (e.g. Jer. 2.2) and twice (e.g. Eccles. 9.1) it is used as the opposite of *misos*, which means *hatred*. *Agapē* has not yet become a great word but there are hints of what is to come. The Book of Wisdom uses it for the love of God (Wisdom 3.9) and for the love of wisdom (Wisdom 6.18). The Letter of Aristeas in talking of beauty says (229) that piety is closely connected with beauty, for 'it is the pre-eminent form of beauty, and its power lies in *love* (*agapē*) which is the gift of God'. Philo uses *agapē* once in its nobler sense. He says that *phobos* (fear) and *agapē* (love) are kindred feelings and that both are characteristic of man's feeling towards God. But we can only find scattered and rare occurrences of this word *agapē*, which is to become the very key word of NT ethics. Now we turn to the verb *agapan*. It occurs oftener in classical Greek than the noun, but it is not very common. It can mean *to greet affectionately*. It can describe the love of money or of precious stones. It can be used for *being content* with some thing or some situation. It is even used once (Plutarch, *Pericles*, 1) to describe a society lady caressing a pet lap-dog. But, the great difference between *philein* and *agapan* in classical Greek is that *agapan* has none of the warmth that characterizes *philein*. There are two good instances of this. Dio Cassius reports Antony's famous speech about Cæsar, and he says (44.48): 'You loved (*philein*) him as a father, and you held him in regard (*agapan*) as a benefactor.' *Philein* describes the warm love for a father; *agapan* describes the affectionate gratitude for a benefactor. In the *Memorabilia* Xenophon describes how Aristarchus took a problem to Socrates. Owing to war conditions he has fourteen female relatives, displaced persons, billeted on him. They have nothing to do and, not unnaturally, there is trouble. Socrates advises him to set them to work, gentlefolk or not. Aristarchus does and the situation is solved. 'There were happy instead of gloomy faces; they loved (*philein*) him as a protector; he regarded them with affection (*agapan*) because they were useful'. (Xenophon,

Memorabilia 2.7.12). Once again there is a warmth in *philein* which is not in *agapan*.

It would not be true to say that the NT never uses anything else but *agapē* and *agapan* to express the Christian love. Some few times *philein* is used. *Philein* is used of the Father's love for the Son (John 5.20); of God's love for men (John 16.27); of the devotion that men ought to bear to Jesus (I Cor. 16.22); but the occurrences of *philein* in the NT are comparatively few, while *agapē* occurs almost 120 times and *agapan* more than 130 times. Before we go on to examine their use in detail, there are certain things about these words and their meaning we must note. We must ask why Christian language abandoned the other Greek words for love and concentrated on these.

It is true to say that all the other words had acquired certain flavours which made them unsuitable. *Erōs* had quite definite associations with the lower side of love; it had much more to do with passion than with love. *Storgē* was very definitely tied up with family affection; it never had in it the width that the conception of Christian love demands.

Philia was a lovely word, but it was definitely a word of warmth and closeness and affection; it could only be properly be used of the near and the dear, and Christianity needed a much more inclusive word than that. Christian thought fastened on this word *agapē* because it was the only word capable of being filled with the content which was required.

The great reason why Christian thought fastened on *agapē* is that *agapē* demands the exercise of the whole man. Christian love must not only extend to our nearest and our dearest, our kith and kin, our friends and those who love us; Christian love must extend to the Christian fellowship, to the neighbour, to the enemy, to all the world.

Now, all the ordinary words for love are words which express an emotion. They are words which have to do with the heart. They express an experience which comes to us unsought, and, in a way, inevitably. We cannot help loving our kith and kin; blood is thicker than water. We speak about *falling in love*. That kind of love is not an achievement; it is something which happens to us and which we cannot help. There is no particular virtue in falling in love. It is something with which we have little or nothing consciously to do; it simply happens. But *agapē* is far more than that.

Agapē has to do with the *mind*: it is not simply an emotion which rises unbidden in our hearts; it is a principle by which we deliberately live. *Agapē* has supremely to do with the *will*. It is a conquest, a victory, an achievement. No one ever naturally loved his enemies. To love one's enemies is a conquest of all our natural inclinations and emotions.

This *agapē*, this Christian love, is not merely an emotional experience which comes to us unbidden and unsought; it is a deliberate principle of the mind, and a deliberate conquest and achievement of the will. It is in fact the power to love the unlovable, to love people whom we do not like. Christianity does not ask us to love our enemies and to love men at large in the same way as we love our nearest and our dearest and those who are closest to us; that would be at one and the same time impossible and wrong. But it does demand that we should have at all times a certain attitude of the mind and a certain direction of the will towards all men, no matter who they are.

What then is the meaning of this *agapē*? The supreme passage for the interpretation of the meaning of *agapē* is Matt. 5.43-48. We are there bidden to love our enemies. Why? *In order that we should be like God.* And what is the typical action of God that is cited? God sends his rain on the just and the unjust and on the evil and the good. That is to say—*no matter what a man is like, God seeks nothing but his highest good.*

Let a man be a saint or let a man be a sinner, God's

only desire is for that man's highest good. Now, that is
what *agape* is. *Agapē* is the spirit which says: 'No matter
what any man does to me, I will never seek to do harm
to him; I will never set out for revenge; I will always seek
nothing but his highest good.' That is to say, Christian love,
agapē, is *unconquerable benevolence, invincible good will.*
It is not simply a wave of emotion; it is a deliberate conviction of the mind issuing in a deliberate policy of the life;
it is a deliberate achievement and conquest and victory of
the will. It takes all of a man to achieve Christian love; it
takes not only his heart; it takes his mind and his will as
well.

If that is so, two things are to be noted.

(i) Human *agapē*, our love towards our fellow men, is
bound to be *a product of the Spirit.* The NT is quite clear
about that (Gal. 5.22; Rom. 15.30; Col. 1.8). Christian *agapē*
is unnatural in the sense that it is not possible for the
natural man. A man can only exercise this universal
benevolence, he can only be cleansed from human hatred
and human bitterness and the natural human reaction to
enmity and injury and dislike, when the Spirit takes
possession of him and sheds abroad the love of God in his
heart.

Christian *agapē* is impossible for anyone except a Christian man. No man can perform the Christian ethic until
he becomes a Christian. He may see quite clearly the
desirability of the Christian ethic; he may see that it is
the solution to the world's problems; mentally he may
accept it; practically he cannot live it, until Christ lives in
him.

(ii) When we understand what *agapē* means, it amply
meets the objection that a society based on this love would
be a paradise for criminals, and that it means simply letting
the evil-doer have his own way. If we seek nothing but a
man's highest good, we may well have to resist a man; we
may well have to punish him; we may well have to do the
hardest things to him—for the good of his immortal soul.

But the fact remains that whatever we do to that man will never be purely vindictive; it will never even be merely retributory; it will always be done in that forgiving love which seeks, not the man's punishment, and still less the man's annihilation, but always his highest good. In other words, *agapē* means treating men as God treats them —and that does not mean allowing them unchecked to do as they like.

When we study the NT we find that love is the basis of every perfect relationship in heaven and in earth.

(i) Love is the basis of the relationship between the Father and the Son, between God and Jesus. Jesus can speak of 'the love wherewith Thou hast loved me' (John 17.26). He is God's 'dear Son' (Col. 1.13; cf. John 3.35; 10.17; 15.9; 17.23, 24)

(ii) Love is the basis of the relationship between the Son and the Father. The purpose of Jesus' whole life was that 'the world may know that he loves the Father' (John 14.31).

(iii) Love is God's attitude to men (John 3.16; Rom. 8.37; Rom. 5.8; Eph. 2.4; II Cor. 13.14; I John 3.1, 16; I John 4.9, 10). Sometimes Christianity is presented in such a way that it looks as if it was the work of a gentle and a loving Jesus to pacify a stern and an angry God, as if Jesus did something which changed the attitude of God to men. The NT knows nothing of that. The whole process of salvation began because God so loved the world.

(iv) It is man's duty to love God (Matt. 22.37; cp. Mark 12.30 and Luke 10.27; Rom. 8.28; I Cor. 2.9; II Tim. 4.8; I John 4.19). Christianity does not think of a man finally submitting to the power of God; it thinks of him as finally surrendering to the love of God. It is not that man's will is crushed, but that man's heart is broken.

(v) The motive power of Jesus' life was love for men (Gal. 2.20; Eph. 5.2; II Thess. 2.16; Rev. 1.5; John 15.9). Jesus is indeed the lover of the souls of men.

(vi) The essence of the Christian faith is love of Jesus

(Eph. 6.24; I Peter 1.8; John 21.15, 16). Just as Jesus is the lover of the souls of men, the Christian is the lover of Christ.

(vii) The mark of the Christian life is the love of Christians for one another (John 13.34; 15.12, 17; I Peter 1.22; I John 3.11, 23; I John 4.7). Christians are people who love Jesus and who love each other.

The basis of every conceivable right relationship in heaven and earth is love. It is on love that all relationships, both human and divine, are founded.

The NT has much to tell us about God's love for men.

(i) Love is the very nature of God. God is love (I John 4.7, 8; II Cor. 13.11).

(ii) God's love is a *universal* love. It was not only a chosen nation, it was the world that God so loved (John 3.16).

(iii) God's love is a *sacrificial* love. The proof of his love is the giving of his Son for men (I John 4.9, 10; John 3.16). The guarantee of Jesus' love is that he loved us and gave himself for us (Gal. 2.20; Eph. 5.2; Rev. 1.5).

(iv) God's love is an *undeserved* love. It was while we were sinners and enemies that God loved us and Jesus died for us (Rom. 5.8; I John 3.1; 4.9,10).

(v) God's love is a *merciful* love (Eph. 2.4). It is not dictatorial, not domineeringly possessive; it is the yearning love of the merciful heart.

(vi) God's love is a *saving* and a *sanctifying* love (II Thess. 2.13). It rescues from the situation of the past and enables men to meet the situations of the future.

(vii) God's love is a *strengthening* love. In it and through it a man becomes more than a conqueror (Rom. 8.37). It is not the softening and over-protective love which makes a man weak and flabby: it is the love which makes heroes.

(viii) God's love is an *inseparable* love (Rom. 8.39). In the nature of things human love must come to an end, at least for a time, but God's love outlasts all the chances and the changes and the threats of life.

(ix) God's love is a *rewarding* love (James 1.12; 2.5). In this life it is a precious thing, and its promises are still greater for the life to come.

(x) God's love is a *chastening* love (Heb. 12.6). God's love is the love which knows that discipline is an essential part of love.

The NT has much to say about what man's love for God must be.

(i) It must be an *exclusive* love (Matt. 6.24; cp. Luke 16.13). There is only room for one loyalty in the Christian life.

(ii) It is a love which is *founded on gratitude* (Luke 7.42, 47). The gifts of God's love demand in return the whole love of our hearts.

(iii) It is an *obedient* love. Repeatedly the NT lays it down that the only way we can prove that we love God is by giving him our unquestioning obedience (John 14.15, 21, 23, 24, 13.35; 15.10; I John 2.5; 5.2, 3; II John 6). Obedience is the final proof of love.

(iv) It is an *outgoing* love. The fact that we love God is proved by the fact that we love and help our fellow men (I John 4.12, 20; 3.14; 2.10). Failure to help men proves that our love of God is unreal and untrue (I John 3.17).

Obedience to God and loving help to men are the two things which prove our love.

We now turn to the other side of the picture—man's love for man.

(i) Love must be the very atmosphere of the Christian life (I Cor. 16.14; Col. 1.4; I Thess. 1.3; 3.6; II Thess. 1.3; Eph. 5.2; Rev. 2.19). Love is the badge of the Christian society. A church where there is bitterness and strife may call itself a church of men, but it has no right to call itself a church of Christ. It has destroyed the atmosphere of the Christian life and is bound to be suffocated; it has lost the badge of the Christian life and is no longer recognizable as a church.

(ii) Love is that by which the Church is built up (Eph.

4.16). It is the cement which holds the Church together; the climate in which the Church can grow; the food which nourishes the Church.

(iii) The motive power of the Christian leader must be love (II Cor. 11.11; 12.15; 2.4; I Tim. 4.12; II Tim. 3.10; II John 1; III John 1). There ought to be no place in the Church for the man who takes office in the Church for the sake of prestige and prominence and power. The motive of the Christian leader must be solely to love and serve God and his fellow-men.

(iv) At the same time the attitude of the Christian to his leaders must be that of love (I Thess. 5.13). Too often that attitude is an attitude of criticism and discontent and even resentment. The bond of the Christian army is the bond of love between those of all ranks within it.

Christian love expands in ever widening circles.

(i) The Christian love begins in the *family* (Eph. 5.25, 28, 33). It is a fact not to be forgotten that a Christian family is one of the finest witnesses in the world to Christianity. Christian love begins at home. The man who has failed to make his own family a centre of Christian love has little right to exercise authority in the wider family of the Church.

(ii) The Christian love goes out to the *brotherhood* (I Peter 2.17). It was the astonished cry of the heathen in the early days, 'See how these Christians love one another.' One of the severest handicaps of the modern Church is that to the outsider it must often appear to be a company of people squabbling bitterly about nothing. A church completely enveloped in the peace of mutual love is a rare phenomenon. Such a church would not be a church where everyone thought the same and agreed on everything; it would be a church in which men could differ and still love each other.

(iii) The Christian love goes out to our *neighbours* (Matt. 19.19; 22.39; cp. Mark 12.31 and Luke 10.27; Rom. 13.9; Gal. 5.14; James 2.8). And the definition of our neighbour is simply that our neighbour is anyone who happens to be in need. As the Roman poet said: ' I regard no human being as a stranger.' It is the simple fact that more people have been brought into the Church by the kindness of real Christian love than by all the theological arguments in the world; and more people have been driven from the Church by the hardness and the ugliness of so-called Christianity than by all the doubts in the world.

(iv) The Christian love goes out to our *enemies* (Luke 6.27; cp. Matt. 5.44). We have seen that Christian love means unconquerable benevolence and invincible good-will. No matter what any man does to him, the Christian will never cease to seek that man's highest good. No matter how he is insulted, injured, wronged and slandered, the Christian will never hate and will never let bitterness into his heart. When Lincoln was accused of treating his opponents with too much courtesy and kindness, and when it was pointed out to him that his whole duty was to destroy them, he answered: ' Do I not destroy my enemies when I make them my friends? ' The Christian's only method of destroying his enemies is to love them into being his friends.

We must now look at the characteristics of this Christian love.

(i) Love is *sincere* (Rom. 12.9; II Cor. 6.6; 8.8; I Peter 1.22). It has no ulterior motive; it is not cupboard love. It is not a surface pleasantness, which cloaks an inner bitterness. It is the love which loves with open eyes and with open heart.

(ii) Love is *innocent* (Rom. 13.10). The Christian love never injured any man. So-called love can injure in two ways. It can lead into sin. Burns said of the man whom he met when he was learning flax-dressing in Irvine: ' His friendship did me a mischief.' Or it can be over-possessive and over-protective. Mother love can become smother love.

(iii) Love is *generous* (II Cor. 8.24). There are two kinds of love—the love which demands and the love which gives. The Christian love is the giving love, because it is a copy of the love of Jesus (John 13.34), and has its mainspring in the giving love of God (I John 4.11).

(iv) Love is *practical* (Heb. 6.10; I John 3.18). It is not merely a kindly feeling, and it does not limit itself to pious good wishes; it is love which issues in action.

(v) Love is *forbearing* (Eph. 4.2). The Christian love is the love which is proof against the things which so easily turn love to hate.

(vi) Love issues in *forgiveness and restoration* (II Cor. 2.8). Christian love is able to forgive, and, in forgiving, it enables the wrong-doer to return to the right way.

(vii) Love is not *sentimental* (II Cor. 2.4). Christian love does not shut its eyes to the faults of others. Love is not blind. It will use rebuke and discipline when these are needed. The love which shuts its eyes to all faults, and which evades the unpleasantness of all discipline, is not real love at all, for in the end it does nothing but harm to the loved one.

(viii) Love *controls liberty* (Gal. 5.13; Rom. 14.15). It is perfectly true that a Christian man has the right to do anything which is not sin. But there are certain things in which a Christian may see no harm, but which may offend other Christians. There are certain things which may do one man no harm, but which may be the ruination of another man. The Christian never forgets his Christian liberty, but he also never forgets that Christian liberty is controlled by Christian love, and by Christian responsibility for others.

(ix) Love *controls truth* (Eph. 4.15). The Christian loves truth (II Thess. 2.10), but he never cruelly or unsympathetically speaks the truth in order to hurt. It was said of Florence Allshorn, the great teacher, that, when she had occasion to rebuke any of her students, she always did it as if with her arm around the person who had to be rebuked. The Christian is never false to the truth, but he always remembers that love and truth must go hand in hand.

(x) Love is *the bond which holds the Christian fellowship together* (Phil. 2.2; Col. 2.2). Paul speaks of Christians being knit together in love. Our theological views may differ; our views on methods may differ. But across the differences there should come the constant memory that we love Christ, and that therefore we love each other.

(xi) Love is *that which gives the Christian the right to ask a help or favour from another Christian* (Philemon 9). If we were really bound together in love as we ought to be, we would find it easy to ask and natural to give when need arose.

(xii) Love is *the motive power of faith* (Gal. 5.6). More people are won for Christ by the appeal to the heart than to the head. Faith is born, not so much from intellectual search, as from the uplifting of the Cross of Christ. It is true that sooner or later we must think things out for ourselves; but in Christianity the heart must feel before the mind can think.

(xiii) Love is *the perfecting of the Christian life* (Rom. 13.10; Col. 3.14; I Tim. 1.5; 6.11; I John 4.12). There is nothing higher in this world than to love. The great task of any church is not primarily to perfect its buildings or its liturgy or its music or its vestments. Its great task is to perfect its love.

Finally, the NT lays it down that there are certain ways in which love can be misdirected.

(i) *Love of the world* is misdirected love (I John 2.15). It was because Demas loved the world that he forsook Paul (II Tim. 4.10). A man can so love time that he forgets eternity. A man can so love the world's prizes that he forgets the ultimate prizes. A man can so love the world that he accepts the world's standards and abandons the standards of Christ.

(ii) *Love of personal prestige* is misdirected love. The scribes and Pharisees loved the chief seats in the synagogues and the praises of men (Luke 11.43; John 12.43). A man's question must always be, not: How does this look to men? but, How does this look to God?

(iii) *Love of the dark* and fear of the light is the inevitable consequence of sin (John 3.19). As soon as a man sins, he has something to hide; and then he loves the dark. But the dark may conceal him from men; it cannot conceal him from God.

So at the end of things we see beyond a doubt that the Christian life is built on the twin pillars of love of God and love of man.

AIŌNIOS

THE WORD OF ETERNITY

W E do well to search out the true meaning of the word *aiōnios*, for in the NT this is the word which is usually translated *eternal* or *everlasting*, and it is applied to the eternal life and the eternal glory, which are the Christian's highest reward, and to the eternal judgment and the eternal punishment, which must be the Christian's greatest dread.

Even in classical and in secular Greek *aiōnios* is a strange word, with a sense of mystery in it. Itself it is an adjective formed from the noun *aiōn*. In classical Greek this word *aiōn* has three main meanings.

(i) It means a *life-time*. Herodotus can speak of ending our *aiōn* (Herodotus, 1.32); Aeschylus, of depriving a man of his *aiōn* (Aeschylus, *Prometheus* 862); and Euripides of breathing away one's *aiōn* (Euripides, *fragment* 801).

(ii) Then it comes to mean an *age*, a *generation*, or an *epoch*. So the Greeks could speak of this present *aiōn*, and of the *aiōn* which is to come, this present age and the age which is to come.

(iii) But then the word comes to mean a *very long space of time*. The prepositional phrase *ap'aiōnos* means *from of old*; and *di'aiōnos* means *perpetually* and *for ever*. It is just here that the first mystery begins to enter in. In the papyri we read how at a public meeting the crowd shout ' The Emperor *eis ton aiōna*, The Emperor *for ever*.'

The adjective *aiōnios* becomes in Hellenistic Greek times the standing adjective to describe the Emperor's power. The royal power of Rome is a power which is to last for ever. And so, as Milligan well puts it, the word *aiōnios* comes to describe ' a state wherein the horizon is not in view'. *Aiōnios* becomes the word of far distances, the word of eternities, the word which transcends time.

But it was Plato who took this word *aiōnios*—he may even have coined it—and gave it its special mysterious meaning. To put it briefly, for Plato *aiōnios* is the word of eternity in contrast with time. Plato uses it, as it has been said, ' to denote that which has neither beginning nor end, and that is subject to neither change nor decay, that which is above time, but of which time is a moving image'.

Plato does not mean by this word simply indefinite continuance—this is a point to which we must later return —but that which is above and beyond time. There are three significant instances of the word in Plato.

In the second book of the *Republic* (363d) Plato is talking of the poets' pictures of heaven. He talks of the rewards Musæus and Eumolpus offer the just men: ' They take them down into the world below, where they have the saints lying on couches at a feast, *everlastingly* drunk, with garlands on their heads; their idea seems to be that an immortality of drunkenness (*aiōnios methē*) is the highest meed of virtue.'

In *The Laws* he speaks of the soul and the body being indestructible, but not *eternal* (904a). There is a difference between simple existence for ever and eternity, for eternity is the possession of gods, not of men.

The most significant of all the Platonic passages is in the *Timæus* 37d. There he speaks about the Creator and the universe which he has created, 'the created glory of the *eternal gods*'—The Creator was glad when he saw his universe, and he wished to make it as nearly like the eternal universe as it could be. But 'to attach eternity to the created was impossible.' So he made time as a moving image of eternity.

The essential point in this picture is that eternity is always the same and always indivisible; in it there is no being created and no becoming; there is no such thing as being older and younger in eternity; there is no past, present or future.

There is no *was* or *will be* but only an eternal *is*. Obviously we cannot have that state in a created world; but none the less the created world is, within its limits, the image of eternity.

Here then is the salient fact. The essence of the word *aiōnios* is that it is the word of the eternal order as contrasted with the order of this world; it is the word of deity as contrasted with humanity; essentially it is the word which can be properly applied to no one other than God. *Aiōnios* is the word which describes nothing less and nothing other than the life of God.

We must now turn to the use of the word *aiōnios* in the NT itself. By far its most important usage there is in connexion with *eternal life*. But that usage is so important that we must retain it for separate treatment. And we must first take a sweeping view of all its usages.

As we do so we must remember that *aiōnios* is distinctively the word of eternity, and that it can properly describe only that which essentially belongs to and befits God.

It is used of the great blessings of the Christian life, blessings which have been brought by Jesus Christ.

It is used of the *eternal covenant* of which Christ is the mediator (Heb. 13.20). A covenant means a relationship with God, and through Jesus Christ men enter into a relationship with God which is as eternal as God himself.

It is used of the *eternal habitations* into which the Christian shall enter (Luke 16.9; II Cor. 5.1). The ultimate destiny of the Christian is a life which is none other than the life of God himself.

It is used of the *eternal redemption* and the *eternal inheritance* into which the Christian enters through Jesus Christ (Heb. 9.15). The safety, the liberty, the release which Christ wrought for men is as lasting as God himself.

It is used of the *glory* into which the faithful Christian will enter (I Peter 5.10; II Cor. 4.17; II Tim. 2.10). There awaits God's faithful man God's own glory.

So it is used in connexion with the words *hope* and *salvation* (Titus 3.7; II Tim. 2.10). There is nothing fleeting, impermanent, destructible about the Christian hope and salvation; even another world could not change or alter them; they are as unchangeable as God himself.

It is used of the *Kingdom of Jesus Christ* (II Peter 1.11). Jesus Christ is not surpassable; he is not a stage on the way; his revelation, his value is the revelation and the value of God himself.

It is used of the *Gospel* (Rev. 14.6). The Gospel is not merely one of many revelations; it is not merely a stage on the way of revelation; it is eternity entered into time.

But while *aiōnios* is used to describe the greatest blessings of the Christian life, it is also used to describe the greatest threats of the Christian life.

It is used to describe the *fire of punishment* (Matt. 18.8; 25.41; Jude 7). It is used to describe *punishment* itself (Matt. 25.46). It is used to describe *judgment* (Heb. 6.2). It is used to describe *destruction* (II Thess. 1.9). It is used to describe the *sin* which finally separates man from God (Mark 3.29).

It is in these passages that we need to be specially careful in our interpretation of the word. Simply to take is as meaning *lasting for ever* is not enough. In all these passages we must remember the essential meaning of *aiōnios*. *Aiōnios* is the word of eternity as opposed to and contrasted with time.

It is the word of deity as opposed to and contrasted with humanity. It is the word which can only really be applied to God. If we remember that, we are left with one tremendous truth—both the blessings which the faithful shall inherit and the punishment which the unfaithful shall receive are *such as befits God to give and to inflict*.

Beyond that we cannot go. Simply to take the word *aiōnios*, when it refers to blessings and punishment, to mean *lasting for ever* is to oversimplify, and indeed to misunderstand, the word altogether. It means far more than that.

It means that that which the faithful will receive and that which the unfaithful will suffer is that which it befits God's nature and character to bestow and to inflict —and beyond that we who are men cannot go, except to remember that that nature and character are holy love.

We must now turn to the greatest of all uses of the word *aiōnios* in the NT, its use in connexion with the phrase *eternal life*. We must begin by reminding ourselves of the fact which we have so often stressed, that the word *aiōnios* is the word of eternity in contrast with time, of deity in contrast with humanity, and that therefore *eternal life is nothing less than the life of God himself*.

(i) The promise of eternal life is the promise that it is open to the Christian to share nothing less than the power and the peace of God himself.

Eternal life is *the promise of God* (Titus 1.2; I John 2.25). God has promised us a share in his own blessedness, and God cannot break a promise.

(ii) But the NT goes further than that—eternal life is not only the promise of God; eternal life is *the gift of God* (Rom. 6.23; I John 5.11). As we shall see, eternal life is not without its conditions; but the fact remains that eternal life is something which God out of his mercy and grace gives to man. It is something which we could neither earn nor deserve; it is the free gift of God to men.

(iii) Eternal life is *bound up with Jesus Christ*. Christ is the living water which is the elixir of eternal life (John 4.14). He is the food which brings to men eternal life (John 6.27, 54). His words are the words of eternal life John 6.68). He himself not only brings (John 17.2, 3) but *is* eternal life (I John 5.20).

If we wish to put this very simply, we may say that through Jesus there is possible a relationship, an intimacy, a unity with God which are possible in no other way. Through what he is and does men may enter into the very life of God himself.

(iv) This eternal life *comes through what the NT calls belief in Jesus Christ* (John 3.15, 16, 36; 5.24; 6.40, 47; I John 5.13; I Tim. 1.16). What does this *belief* mean? Clearly it is not simply intellectual belief. Belief in Jesus means that we believe absolutely and implicitly that what Jesus says about God is true.

If we really believe that God is Father and that God is love, that God cares enough for men to send his Son into the world to die for them, it literally makes all the difference in the world to life, for it means that life is in the hands of the love of God. But further, this belief means believing that Jesus is who he claims to be.

Obviously the reliance that we can place on any statement depends entirely on the position of the person who makes it. We are bound to ask : How can I believe for sure that what Jesus tells me about God is true? The answer is that we believe what Jesus tells us about God, because we believe that Jesus has a unique right to speak about God, because we believe that Jesus is the Son of God. Therefore we enter into eternal life by believing that Jesus is the Son of God.

But belief goes even further than that. We believe that God is Father and that God is love, because we believe that Jesus, being the Son of God, has told us the truth about

God—*and then we act on that belief*. We live life in the
certainty that we can do nothing other than render a
perfect trust and a perfect obedience to God.

Eternal life is nothing else than the life of God himself.
We enter into that life through believing in Jesus Christ.
That belief involves three elements.

(i) It involves believing that God is the kind of God
Jesus told men about.

(ii) It involves the certainty that Jesus is the Son of
God, and therefore has the right to speak about God in a
way that no one else ever could or ever will be able to
speak.

(iii) It involves living all life on the assumption that
these things are true. When we do that, we share nothing
less than the life of God, the power and the peace which
God alone can give.

We have already said that eternal life is the gift of God;
all God's gifts are freely given, but they are not given away.
They are there for the taking, but they must be taken.

Let us use a human analogy. All the beauty and the
wealth and the loveliness and the wisdom of classical
literature are there for any man to take; but before he can
enter into them, he must undergo the work, the study and
the discipline which the learning of Latin and Greek
demands.

God's offer of eternal life is there; but man must claim
it and enter into it before he can receive it.

(i) Eternal life demands *knowledge of God*. Eternal life
means ' to know the only true God ' (John 17.3). Now man
can only know God through three avenues. He must use
his mind to think; he must use his eyes to see and his
heart to love Jesus Christ; he must use his ears to listen to
what God is seeking to say to him.

If we are to enter into life eternal we must never be too
busy with the things of time to think about the eternal
things, to walk looking unto Jesus, and to be regularly in
a listening silence wherein we wait upon God.

(ii) Eternal life demands *obedience to God*. God's commandment is eternal life (John 12.50). Jesus is the author of eternal salvation to all that obey him (Heb. 5.9). Only in doing his will is our peace.

God's pleading is with the rebellious; but God's gifts are for the obedient. We can never enter into complete intimacy and unity with someone from whom we continually differ, and whom we continually grieve by our disobedience. Obedience to God and eternal life from God go hand in hand.

(iii) Eternal life is the reward of *strenuous loyalty* (I Tim. 6.12). It comes to the man who has fought the good fight of faith and who has clung to Christ through thick and thin. Eternal life comes to the man who *hears and follows* (John 10.27, 28).

No man who goes his own way can enter into eternal life; eternal life is for the man who in complete loyalty takes the way of Jesus Christ.

(iv) There is an *ethical demand in eternal life*. Eternal life is the goal of the way of holiness (Rom. 6.22). It comes to those who show patient continuance in well-doing (Rom. 2.7). It cannot come to the man who hates his brother, and who is therefore in his heart a murderer (I John 3.15). It comes to those who keep themselves in the love of God (Jude 21).

There is no escaping the ethical demand of Christianity. Eternal life is not for the man who does as he likes; it is for the man who does as Jesus Christ likes. It is not a case of demanding that we should be perfect; but it is a case of demanding that, however often we fall and fail, we should still fasten our eyes on Jesus Christ.

(v) Eternal life is the reward of *the labourer for Christ* (John 4.36). Eternal life is promised to the man who helps Jesus Christ to reap the harvest of the souls of men. Eternal life is God's offer to the man who is more concerned to save others than selfishly to save his own soul.

(vi) Eternal life is the reward of the *adventurer of*

Christ (John 12.25). It is for the man who hates his life and who is prepared to throw it away for the sake of Jesus Christ. It is for the man who is ever ready 'to venture for thy name'. It is for the man who accepts the risks of the Christian life, and who is prepared 'to bet his life that there is a God'.

(vii) Eternal life is the result of that *righteousness which comes through the grace of Jesus Christ* (Rom. 5.21). The essential meaning of righteousness is a new relationship with God through that which Jesus Christ has done for us.

And so we end where we began—eternal life is the life of God himself, and into that life we, too, may enter when we accept what Jesus Christ has done for us, and what he tells us about God.

We shall never enter into the full ideas of eternal life until we rid ourselves of the almost instinctive assumption that eternal life means primarily life which goes on for ever. Long ago the Greeks saw that such a life would be by no means necessarily a blessing.

They told the story of Aurora, the goddess of dawn, who fell in love with Tithonus, the mortal youth. Zeus offered her any gift she might choose for her mortal lover. She asked that Tithonus might never die; but she forgot to ask that he might remain for ever young. So Tithonus lived for ever growing older and older and more and more decrepit, till life became a terrible and intolerable curse.

Life is only of value when it is nothing less than the life of God—and that is the meaning of eternal life.

AKOLOUTHEIN

THE DISCIPLE'S WORD

AKOLOUTHEIN is the common and normal Greek verb which means *to follow*. It is a word with many uses and

with many associations and all of them add something to
its meaning for the follower of Christ. First, let us look at
its usage and its meaning in classical Greek.

(i) It is the common and the usual word for *soldiers
following their leader and commander*. Xenophon (*Anabasis* 7.5.3) speaks about the generals and captains who have
followed the leader for whom they are fighting.

(ii) It is very commonly used of a slave *following* or
attending his master. Theophrastus, in his character sketch
of the Distrustful Man, says that such a man compels his
slave to walk before him instead of following behind him,
as a slave would normally do, so that he can be sure the
slave will not dodge away (Theophrastus, *Characters* 18.8).

(iii) It is commonly used of *following* or *obeying* someone else's advice or opinion. Plato says that it is necessary
to find out those who are fitted by nature to be leaders in
philosophy and government, and those who are fitted by
nature to be followers of the leader (Plato, *Republic* 474c).
Some people are fitted to give leadership; others are only
fitted to accept it.

(iv) It is commonly used of *obeying* the laws. To *follow*
the laws of a city is to accept them as the standard of life
and of behaviour.

(v) It is commonly used of *following the thread or argument of a discourse*. When the argument has got into a
difficult position Socrates says: 'Come now, try to *follow*
me, to see if we can get this matter adequately explained'
(Plato, *Republic* 474c).

(vi) In the papyri *akolouthein* is very commonly used for
attaching oneself to someone in order to extract some
favour which is desired. One writes in advice to another:
'*Stick to* Ptollarion all the time. . . . *Stick to* him so that
you may become his friend.' The idea is that of following a
person until the favour desired is finally extracted from
him.

Every one of these usages has light to throw on the
Christian life.

The Christian is in the position of the soldier who follows Jesus Christ, and who must immediately obey his leader's command.

The Christian is in the position of the slave, who must obey as soon as his master speaks.

The Christian must ask for the advice and for the ruling of Jesus Christ and must have the humility to follow it, whatever it may be.

The Christian is the man who desires citizenship of the Kingdom of Heaven, and, if he is to receive it, he must agree to live according to its laws.

The Christian is the learner and the listener who must listen to the words of Jesus, and who must follow their thread, so that day by day he may learn more of the wisdom which Jesus is ever wishing to teach him.

The Christian is always in the position of one who needs and desires the favour and the grace and the help which Jesus Christ can give to him, and who follows Christ because in Christ alone he finds his need supplied.

We now turn to the use of *akolouthein* in the NT itself. It is very frequent there.

(i) It is used of the disciples who left their various trades and occupations and *followed* Jesus. So it is used of Peter and Andrew (Mark 1.18; cp. Matt. 4.20). It is used of the two disciples of John the Baptist who *followed* Jesus when John pointed at Jesus as the Lamb of God (John 1.37). It is used of the reaction of the disciples after the miraculous catch of fishes; they forsook all and *followed* Jesus (Luke 5.11). It is the claim of the disciples towards the end that they have left everything to *follow* Jesus (Matt. 19.27). It is used of the would-be disciples whom Jesus told to think again before they launched out on the adventure of following him (Matt. 8.19; cp. Luke 9.59, 61).

(ii) It is the word which Jesus used to summon men to himself. On Jesus' lips it is the word of challenge. His commandment to Matthew is: *Follow* me (Mark 2.14; cp. Luke 5.27; Matt. 9.9). It is Jesus' command to Philip (John

1.43). It is his final command to Peter (John 21.19, 22). It is his unaccepted command to the Rich Young Ruler (Matt. 19.21; cp. Luke 18.22). His command to all his would-be followers is that they should take up their cross and *follow* him (Mark 8.34; 10.21; Matt. 10.38; 16.24; Luke 9.23).

(iii) Most commonly of all this word is used of the crowds who *followed* Jesus (Matt. 4.25; 8.1; 12.15; 14.13; 19.2; 20.9; 21.9; Mark 3.7; 5.24; 11.9; John 6.2). This use is very closely connected with the usage of the verb in the papyri to describe the act of attaching oneself to someone until a request is granted. Sometimes the crowds followed Jesus to experience his healing power; sometimes they followed him to listen to his words; and sometimes, towards the end, they followed him in wondering admiration to see what was going to happen to him. Another instance of this use of *akolouthein* in the sense of following to receive a favour is Matt. 9.27, when the two blind men are said to follow Jesus in order that he might heal them.

(iv) Sometimes the following is the result of gratitude. In Matt. 20.34 the two blind men are said to *follow* Jesus after they had received their sight; the same is said of the blind man in Luke 18.43; and of Bartimæus in Mark 10.52. They followed because they were drawn with the cords of gratitude for what Jesus had done.

(v) In Mark 2.15 it is said that the sinners *followed* Jesus. That is a most significant usage. There was that about Jesus which they knew would meet their need; they would have avoided a Pharisee, but Jesus they followed, because they knew that he knew and understood their case.

We can distinguish in these uses of *akolouthein* five reasons for following Jesus.

(i) The disciples followed Jesus because of the sheer compelling attraction of his summons.

(ii) The crowds followed Jesus because they desired the things which he alone could give them.

(iii) The sinners followed Jesus because they felt that he

alone could enable them to mend their broken lives and to begin again.

(iv) The blind men followed Jesus that they might receive their sight. They desired to experience his wonder-working power.

(v) The blind men whose eyes were opened followed Jesus in sheer gratitude for what he had done for them.

There we see in summary the motives of the approach of the heart to Jesus Christ.

It will repay us still further to study the usages of *akolouthein* in the gospels.

1. We must see what following Jesus *involves*.

(i) Following Jesus involves *counting the cost*. In Luke 9.59, 61, Jesus seems actually to discourage people from following him until he has made quite sure that they know what they are doing. Jesus does not want anyone to follow him on false pretences, nor will he accept an emotional and easily-moved offer of an unconsidered service.

(ii) Following Jesus involves *sacrifice*. Repeatedly it is pointed out what people left to follow him (Luke 5.11; Matt. 4.20, 22; 19.27). The real point for us there is that following Jesus is what in modern language is called a whole-time job. But there is this difference for us—that following Jesus involves for us serving him within our work, and not by leaving it. In many cases it would be far easier to leave it; but our duty is to witness for him where he has sent us.

(iii) Following Jesus involves a *cross* (Matt. 16.24; cp. Mark 8.34 and Luke 9.23). The real reason for that is that no man can follow Jesus and ever again do what he likes. To follow Jesus may well mean the sacrifice of the pleasures, habits, aims, ambitions which have woven themselves into our lives. Following Jesus always involves this act of surrender—and surrender is never easy.

2. We must see what following Jesus *gives*. In this direction there are two great promises from the Fourth Gospel.

(i) To follow Jesus means to walk not in the darkness, but in the light (John 8.12). When a man walks by himself he walks in the darkness of uncertainty, and he may well end in the darkness of sin. To walk with Jesus is to be sure of the way, and in his company to be safe.

(ii) To follow Jesus is to be certain of ultimately arriving at the glory where he himself is (John 12.26). This is the other side of the warning that to follow Jesus means a sacrifice and a cross. The sacrifice and the cross are not pointless. They are the price of the eternal glory. Jesus never promised an easy way, but he did promise a way in the end of which the hardness of the way would be forgotten.

3 We must see that there are *inadequate* ways of following Jesus. These ways are not to be condemned. They are infinitely better than nothing, but they are not the best.

(i) At the end Peter followed Jesus *afar off* (Matt. 26.58; cp. Mark 14.54 and Luke 22 54). The real reason was that Peter did not dare to follow any nearer; and the real tragedy is that if Peter had kept close to Jesus, the disaster of his denial might never have happened, for it was when Peter saw Jesus' face again that he discovered what he had done by his repeated denials.

(ii) On the last journey to Jerusalem the disciples followed *afraid* (Mark 10.32). In a way that was the bravest act of all. They did not understand what was happening; they feared the worst; and yet they followed him. We can take comfort from reminding ourselves that often the man who follows Christ in fear and trembling is showing the highest courage of all.

4. Lastly we must note that a man can *refuse* to follow Jesus. That is what the Rich Young Ruler did (Matt. 19.21; cp. Luke 18.22). The result of his refusal was that he went away sorrowful. The result of refusal is always sorrow; the result of following, however hard and frightening the way, is always joy.

ALAZŌN AND ALAZONEIA

THE WORDS OF THE EMPTY BOAST

THE word *alazōn* occurs twice in the NT, in Rom. 1.30 and II Tim. 3.2. In both places the AV translates it *boasters* and Moffatt *boastful*.

The word *alazoneia* also occurs twice in the NT, in James 4.16 and I John 2.16. In the James passage the AV translates it *boastings*, and Moffatt *proud pretensions*. In the I John passage the AV translates it by the famous phrase *the pride of life*, and Moffatt translates it *the proud glory of life*.

These words have behind them a most interesting picture, which makes them all the more vivid and meaningful. The Greeks derived them from *alē*, which means *a wandering about*; and an *alazōn* was one of these wandering quacks who could be found shouting their wares in every market-place and in every fair-ground, and offering to sell men their patent cure-alls.

Plutarch, for instance, uses it to describe a *quack doctor* (Plutarch, *Moralia* 523). It was the word for these quacks and cheapjacks who travelled the country and set up their stalls wherever crowds gathered, to sell their patent pills and potions, and to boast that they could cure anything.

So in Greek the word came to mean *a pretentious braggart*. The Platonic Definitions define *alazoneia* as ' the claim to good things which a man does not really possess'.

Aristotle defines the *alazōn* as the man ' who pretends to praiseworthy qualities which he does not possess, or possesses in a lesser degree than he makes out' (Aristotle, *Nicomachean Ethics* 1127a 21). Again in the *Rhetoric* (1384a 6) he says that ' it is the sign of *alazoneia* to claim that things it does not possess belong to it'.

Plato uses the word *alazōn* to describe the 'false and boastful words' which can get into a young man's mind and drive out 'the pursuits and true words which are the best guardians and sentinels in the minds of men who are dear to the gods' (Plato, *Republic* 560c).

In the *Gorgias* Plato draws a picture of the souls of men before the judge in the afterworld, souls 'where every act has left its smirch, where all is awry through falsehood and imposture, *alazoneia*, and nothing straight because of a nurture that knew not the truth' (Plato, *Gorgias* 525a).

Xenophon tells how Cyrus the Persian king, who knew men, defined the *alazōn*: 'The name *alazōn* seems to apply to those who pretend that they are richer than they are, or braver than they are, and to those who promise to do what they cannot do, and that, too, when it is evident that they do this only for the sake of getting something or making some gain' (Xenophon, *Cyropaedia* 2.2.12).

In the *Memorabilia* he tells how Socrates utterly condemned such impostors. Socrates said they are are found in every walk of life, but they were worst of all in politics. 'Much the greatest rogue of all, is the man who has gulled his city into the belief that he is fit to direct it' (Xenophon, *Memorabilia* 1.7.5).

Theophrastus has a famous character sketch of the *alazōn*. '*Alazoneia*', he begins, 'would seem to be, in fact, pretension to advantages which one does not possess'. The *alazōn* is the man who will stand in the market-place and talk to strangers about the argosies he has at sea and his vast trading enterprises when his bank balance is precisely tenpence! He will tell of the campaigns he served with Alexander the Great, and how he was on terms of personal intimacy with him.

He will talk about the letters which the chiefs of the state write to him for help and advice. When he is living in lodgings he will pretend that the house in which his room is situated is the family mansion, and that he is thinking of selling it because it is not commodious enough for the entertaining which he has to do (Theophrastus, *Characters* 23).

The *alazōn* was the braggart and the boaster out to impress men; the man with all his goods in the shop window; the man given to making extravagant claims which he can never fulfil. But we have still to see the *alazōn* in his most damaging and dangerous form.

It was not so very dangerous for a man to lay claim to a business or a fortune which he did not possess; but in the days of the NT there were men who made claims which were exceedingly dangerous.

These men were the Sophists. The Sophists were Greek wandering teachers who claimed to sell knowledge; and, in effect, the knowledge they claimed to sell was the knowledge of how to be a success in life. The Greeks loved words; and the Sophists claimed to give men subtle skill in words, so that, in the famous phrase ' they could make the worse appear the better reason '. They claimed to give men that magic of words which would make the orator the master of men.

Aristophanes pillories them in *The Clouds*. He says the whole object of their teaching was to teach men to fascinate the jury, to win impunity to cheat, and to find an argument to justify anything. Isocrates, the great Greek teacher, hated them. ' They merely try,' he said, ' to attract pupils by low fees and big promises' (Isocrates, *Sophist* 10. 193a).

He said: ' They make impossible offers, promising to impart to their pupils an exact science of conduct by means of which they will always know what to do. Yet for this science they charge only £15 or £20. . . . They try to attract pupils by the specious titles of the subjects which they claim to teach, such as Justice and Prudence.

' But the Justice and Prudence which they teach are of a very peculiar sort, and they give a meaning to the words quite different from that which ordinary people give; in fact they cannot be sure about the meaning themselves, but can only dispute about it. Although they profess to teach justice, they refuse to trust their pupils, and make them deposit the fees with a third party before the course begins' (Isocrates, *Sophist* 4. 291d).

Plato savagely attacks them in his book called *The Sophist* : 'Hunters after young men of wealth and position, with sham education as their bait, and a fee for their object, making money by a scientific use of quibbles in private conversation, while quite aware that what they are teaching is wrong.'

It is these men, and the like of them, of whom the NT is thinking, and against whom it warns the Christian. The warning is against the false teacher who claims to teach men the truth, and who does not know it himself. The world is still full of these people who offer men a so-called wisdom, who shout their wares wherever men meet, who claim to have the cure and the solution to everything. How can we distinguish these men?

(i) Their characteristic is *pride*. In the *Testament of Joseph*, Joseph tells how he treated his brethren : 'My land was their land, and their counsel my counsel. And I exalted myself not among them in *arrogance* (*alazoneia*) because of my worldly glory, but I was among them as one of the least' (*Testament of Joseph* 17.8). The *alazōn* is the teacher who struts as he teaches, and who is fascinated by his own cleverness.

(ii) Their stock in trade is *words*. The Sophist defended himself to Epictetus that the young men came to him looking for someone to teach them. 'To teach them to live?' demands Epictetus. And then he answers his own question : 'No, fool; not how to live, but how to talk; which is also the reason why he admires you' (Epictetus, *Discourses* 3.23). The *alazōn* seeks to substitute clever words for fine deeds.

(iii) Their motive is *profit*. The *alazōn* is out for what he can get. Prestige for his reputation and money for his

pocket is his aim. The program he preaches is designed
to return his party to power and himself to office.

The *alazōn* is not dead. There are still the teachers who
offer worldly cleverness instead of heavenly wisdom; who
spin fine words which never end in any lovely action;
whose teaching is aimed at self-advancement and whose
desire is profit and power.

ELPIS AND ELPIZEIN

THE CHRISTIAN HOPE

THE noun *elpis* means *hope*, and the verb *elpizein* means
to hope. These words are not of any particular linguistic
interest. Their great interest lies in the fact that if we
examine and analyse their use in the NT we can discover
the content and the basis of the Christian hope.

Elpis, *hope*, is one of the three great pillars of the
Christian faith. It is on *hope*, along with faith and love,
that the whole Christian faith is founded (1 Cor. 13.13).
Hope is characteristically the Christian virtue and it is
something which for the non-Christian is impossible (Eph.
2.12). Only the Christian can be an optimist regarding the
world. Only the Christian can hope to cope with life. And
only the Christian can regard death with serenity and
equanimity.

Let us then see in what this Christian hope consists.

(i) It is the *hope of the resurrection of the dead*. That
thought runs consistently all through the NT (Acts 23.6;
26.6; I Thess. 4.13; I Peter 1.3; I John 3.3; I Cor. 15.19). The
Christian is a man who is on his way, not to death, but to
life. For him death is not the abyss of nothingness and
annihilation. It is 'the gate on the skyline'.

(ii) It is *the hope of the glory of God* (Rom. 5.2). It is
the hope that no longer shall we see the glory of God in

the cloud and through a glass darkly. It is the certainty that the day will come when we shall see and be clothed with the glory of God.

(iii) It is *the hope of a new dispensation* (II Cor. 3.12). So long as men regarded themselves as governed by law, there was room for nothing but despair, for there is none who can obey and satisfy the perfect law of God. But when we see that the key-note of religion is not law but love a new hope is born.

(iv) It is *the hope of righteousness* (Gal. 5.5). In Paul *righteousness* or *justification* means *a right relationship with God*. When a man regards religion as law he must be ever in default before God, and therefore ever in terror of God. But the message of Jesus Christ enables a man to enter into a new relationship with God where the terror is gone and where childlike confidence takes its place.

(v) It is *the hope of salvation*. This has two aspects. (a) It is the confidence of safety in this world (II Cor. 1.10), not in the sense of protection from trouble and danger, but in the sense of independence of them. As Rupert Brooke wrote,

Safe shall be my going,
Secretly armed against all death's endeavour;
Safe though all safety's lost; safe where men fall;
And if these poor limbs die, safest of all.

(b) It is the confidence of safety in the world to come. It is the hope of safety amidst the perils of earth, and rescue from the judgment of God.

(vi) It is *the hope of eternal life* (Titus 1.2; 3.7). In the NT the word *eternal* always stresses, not the *duration*, but the *quality* of life. *Eternal* is the word which describes anything which is *proper to God*. Eternal life is the kind of life God lives. The hope of the Christian is that some day he will share the very life of God.

(vii) It is *the hope of the triumphant Second Coming of Christ* (Titus 2.13; I Peter 1.13; 1 John 3.3). The Second Coming is not a fashionable doctrine to-day, but it does conserve this great truth—*that history is going somewhere*, that history is not a knotless thread, and a haphazard collection of meaningless and disconnected events. There is a consummation. The Christian is a man who regards himself and all life as being on the way to a goal.

(viii) It is *a hope which is laid up in heaven* (Col. 1.5). That is to say, it looks forward to something which is already prepared for the Christian, and that something is not something which is at the mercy of the chances and the changes of time. It is in the keeping of God, and therefore it is something which will be the completing of God's design and the fulfilment of all the hopes and dreams of the soul of man.

We may now look at what we may call the sources of hope, or the springs of hope.

(i) Hope is the product of experience (Rom. 5.4). It may be that the experiences and the testings of life drive the non-Christian to despair. The Christian has a hope which sees all things and which grows ever brighter and not dimmer.

(ii) Hope is the product of the Scriptures (Rom. 15.4). If a man will study the record of God's dealings with men and God's intention for men it will leave him full of hope. Oliver Cromwell, in planning his son Richard's education, said, 'I would have him learn a little history.' For the Christian the lesson of history is hope.

(iii) Hope comes from the sense of being called by God (Eph. 1.18). The Christian has not the despairing sense of a salvation into which he must struggle. Such a struggle would be hopeless. He has the sense of a new relationship with God into which he has been invited, not because he deserved it, but by the sheer mercy of God.

(iv) Hope is the product of the gospel (Col. 1.23). The gospel is good news. A message like the message of John the

Baptist (Luke 3.7, 17) is a message with a threat that would drive any man to despair. The message of Jesus is an invitation, an offer, a promise, a piece of startling good news which will lift up the heart of any man who is haunted by his sin.

(v) Hope is dependent on Jesus and on his work (Col. 1.27; I Tim. 1.1). The Christian hope is not founded on anything that a man has done, or can do, for himself. It is founded on what Christ has done for him.

Now let us gather together certain great things which happen by hope.

(i) Hope comes through grace (II Thess. 2.16). The very foundation of Christian hope is the free and undeserved offer of forgiveness and fellowship that God offers to men. Hope is born when we discover that we do not *earn* salvation, but *receive* it.

(ii) It is through hope that we rejoice (Rom. 12.12). A gloomy Christian is a contradiction in terms. The man who knows the power of Christ can never again despair about himself or about the world. He has discovered what Cavour called 'the sense of the possible', for he has discovered that all things are possible with God.

(iii) We are saved by hope (Rom. 8.24). The hope that God is as Jesus said he was is the basis of all salvation. It is not until we begin to see God as the God and Father of our Lord Jesus Christ that we can even contemplate salvation as a possibility for sinful man.

(iv) Hope keeps the Christian steadfast. This is one of the great key-notes of the letter to the Hebrews (Heb. 3.6; 6.11, 18). The Christian is the man who can battle and struggle on, who can fight against himself and his temptations, who can endure the hardness of being a Christian, because he has something infinitely precious to look forward to.

Lastly, let us look at what we may call the foundations of hope.

(i) Hope is in Christ (I Thess. 1.3). We hope, not because

of any strength that we can bring to life, but because we are now sure of the help that Christ can bring.

(ii) Hope is grounded in God (I Tim. 4.10), for God is the God of hope (Rom. 15.13). God is the God who gives hope. The character of God as Jesus told it to us is the ultimate ground of all our hope.

(iii) Hope looks to God. It faces God (Acts 24.15; I Peter 1.21; 3.5; I Tim. 5.5). The Christian is the man of hope because he keeps his eyes fixed on God. Augustine told a wretched man who thought of nothing but his sins, 'Look away from yourself and look to God.' The Godward look is the secret of the Christian hope.

The Christian hope is not simply a trembling, hesitant hope that perhaps the promises of God may be true. It is the confident expectation that they cannot be anything else than true.

ENERGEIA, ENERGEIN, ENERGĒMA, ENERGES

DIVINE POWER IN ACTION

IT is quite clear to anyone that these Greek words have in them the root of our English word *energy*. In the NT they are never used to describe any human power. Always they describe the action of some power which is beyond the power of man and the power of this world. On certain infrequent occasions they describe the action of a malignant power, demonic, and hostile to God; but far more frequently they describe the action of God himself.

They are therefore very important words, for through them we shall learn something of the power of God in action in Christ, in the world, and in the lives of men.

These words came into Christianity with a long and an important history and their history goes a long way

towards helping us to understand their Christian flavour
and usage. So then, first of all, let us study their usage in
classical Greek.

We may best get at their classical meaning by studying
the word *energos,* which does not occur in the NT at all,
but which has in it the germs of all the other meanings.
Energos is an adjective.

In Xenophon's *Memorabilia* (1.4.4) there is a passage
where Socrates is discussing the actions of a man who was
prepared to reverence the great writers and the great artists,
but who was not prepared to reverence the gods. 'Which
do you think,' he demands, 'deserve the greater admiration,
the creators of phantoms without sense and motion, or the
creators of living, intelligent, *active (energos)* human
beings?' *Energos* describes that which is radiantly and
vividly *alive.*

Herodotus (8.26) tells of certain Arcadian deserters who
came to the Persians, because they were in need of food
and wished *to be employed (energos). Energos* describes
action in opposition to inaction.

Energos is used to describe someone who is *on duty.*
Plato in *The Laws* (674b) lays it down : 'Magistrates, during
their year of office, and pilots and judges, while *on duty,*
should taste no wine at all.' *Energos* describes a man *on
duty* in his profession or calling.

Energos frequently has a military connexion. Thucydides
speaks on one occasion of the Athenian fleet as having
the largest number of ships the Athenians ever had *on
active service (energos)* (Thucydides, 3.17).

Xenophon tells how Cyrus made an example of certain
men, and said that such men must be weeded out, if we are
to keep our army *energos, industrious, efficient, fit for
active service* (Xenophon, *Cyropaedia* 2.2.23). Polybius uses
energos to describe a *vigorous* attack (4.63.8); an *effective*
weapon (1.40.12); a march made *with rapidity* (5.8.34).

Energos is frequently used of land which is *cultivated*
and therefore *productive.* Plutarch speaks of a plain *produc-*

ing enough to feed tens of thousands (*Caesar* 58). He speaks
of the law of Peisistratus against idleness ' in consequence of
which the country became more *productive* (*energos*) and
the city more tranquil' (*Solon* 31). Xenophon uses *energos*
to describe *cultivated* as opposed to uncultivated land.

Energos is used to describe a mine which produces
minerals and which is not worked out. It is used of money,
capital, which is not lying idle but which is put out to
produce interest. In the papyri *energos* is used to describe a
mill which is *in working order*. The Septuagint uses *energos*
for a *working day* as opposed to the Sabbath when work
was forbidden (Ezek. 46.1).

Here then we have a whole series of ideas, all of which
have something to contribute to the NT usage of these
words. These words have the meaning of vitality as
opposed to deadness, activity as opposed to idleness, efficiency as opposed to uselessness, effective activity as
opposed to ineffectiveness. All these ideas will light up the
conception of the divine activity of God.

But before we go on to study the NT uses of the words,
we must look at the other words in their classical usage.

Let us next look at the word *energeia* in its classical
usage. *Energeia* is a noun meaning *activity* or *operation*. As
we shall go on to see, this activity and operation have a
special flavour.

Aristotle (*Rhetoric* 1141b 28) uses *energeia* to describe
vigour of style. In Greek grammar *energeia* has one technical meaning; it means the *active* mood of the verb in
contradistinction to the *passive*. *Energeia* is used of the
massive force of a siege engine, a battering-ram (Diodorus
Siculus, 20.95). It is used of the actual *performance* of the
duties which befit a man (Philodemus, 1.91).

Galen the medical writer has two interesting and significant usages of the word. He describes it as 'the action
which is productive of a result' (*On the Natural Faculties*
1.2, 4, 5). And he uses it (*Works*, ed. Kuhn, Vol. 6, p. 647) of
the action or the activity of a drug or a medicine, in the

same sense as we speak of a drug *acting* or *working*.

Already one thing becomes clear. The whole tone of *energeia* is *effective action*; it is not simply *action*; it is always action which issues in the desired and purposed result.

Aristotle has a very significant usage of *energeia*, a usage which is characteristic of his ethical writings. He uses *energeia* of that which is *actual* in contradistinction to that which is only *potential*. A man may appear to have all the gifts and all the talents, but they may be only potential; they may be there, but they may never emerge in effective action; it is only when these gifts and talents become actual, become manifested in action, that *energeia* exists.

In the *Nicomachean Ethics* he writes (1098b 33): 'It no doubt makes a great difference whether we conceive the Supreme Good to depend on possessing virtue, or displaying it—on disposition, or on the manifestation of a disposition *in action*' (*energeia*).

He writes (1101a 15): 'May we not then confidently pronounce that man happy who realizes complete virtue *in action?*' (*energein*). He writes (1098a 16): 'The good of a man is *the exercise* of his soul's faculties in conformity with virtue and excellence.'

Here is something very suggestive. *Energeia* is not a man's potential action; it is his actual action. *Energeia* is the demonstration of inner character in deeds. It is goodness plus efficiency, which indeed is the most effective force in the world. It is not simply energy; it is not misdirected energy; it is not ineffective energy; it is focussed, purposeful, meaningful, effective, energetic action.

In classical Greek the word *energein* has all the characteristics of its kindred noun *energeia*. It means *to be in action* or *to operate*, but always with the idea of effectiveness behind it. As we have seen, Aristotle uses it of the effective action of virtue in contradistinction to the unrealized potential of virtue. Polybius (1.13.5) uses it of the energetic and effective carrying on of a campaign.

It has two technical medical usages. It is used of *the efficacious action* of a drug; and it is the technical Greek word for *to operate* in surgery. *Energein* has the twin ideas of action and of effective action, of action, and of action which achieves its desired result.

The noun *energēma* means *action, activity* or *operation.* It means something actively done, in contradistinction to something merely suffered, endured or experienced. Perhaps its most suggestive use is that it is used of the Labours of Hercules, a series of labours undertaken and brought to a successful conclusion.

Energēs is the NT form of the classical adjective *energos.* In classical Greek it is not common, but when it does occur it means *effective.* It is used of drugs which are effective; and it is used of siege engines which can breach the walls of a city which is attacked.

The more we study this group of words, the more the same idea keeps recurring, the idea of action, strong and powerful, and above all effective. Again and again the idea of power and the idea of purpose achieved meet in these words. And that is most suggestive when we go on to see that in the NT these are the characteristic words for the action of God.

Energeia occurs in the NT nine times, and always in the writings of Paul. In Eph. 1.19 he speaks of the *working* of God's mighty power, which wrought in Christ, when he raised him from the dead. In Eph. 3.7 Paul says that his ministry was given him by the grace of God by the *effectual working* of his power.

In Eph. 4.16 he describes the body of the Church, harmoniously compounded together, according to the *effectual working* in the measure of every part. In Phil. 3.21 Paul speaks of his certainty that Jesus Christ will change the body of our humiliation into the body of his glory, according to the *working* whereby he is able to subdue all things to himself.

In Col. 1.29 Paul speaks of his own preaching in which

he strives according to God's *working*, which *worketh* (*energein*) mightily in him. In Col. 2.12 he speaks of the Christian being buried with Christ in baptism, and raised to life anew, through faith of the *operation* of God, which raised Christ from the dead.

In II Thessalonians we find two of the references to the evil, demonic, anti-God power. In 2.9 we read of the *working* of Satan displayed in the signs and wonders which anti-Christ can work; and in 2.11 we read of an *energeia* of delusion, sent by God upon unbelievers.

The word *energein* occurs in the NT about 19 times. It is three times used of the evil and the demonic power. It is used in Rom. 7.5 of the passions of sin *working* in our members to produce death. In Eph. 2.2 it is used of the spirit that *works* in the children of disobedience. In II Thess. 2.7 it is used of the *working* of the mystery of iniquity.

Far oftener it is used of the working of the power of God. It is used of the miraculous power which *worked* in the miracles of Jesus (Matt. 14.2; cp. Mark 6.14), and which still *works* in the miracles of the Church (Gal. 3.5), and in the gifts and graces which are the equipment and adornment of the Christian life.

It is used of the power which works within the Christian life. Eph. 3.20 speaks of the power that *worketh in us*. Phil. 2.13 speaks of God who *works in us* both to know and to do of his good pleasure.

It is used of the working out of the Christian life. Salvation is *worked out*, made *effective*, by endurance (II Cor. 1.6). It is used of God's power in the ministry of his preachers. The God who *worked* in Paul to make him an apostle to the Gentiles did so in Peter to make him an apostle to the Jews (Gal. 2.8).

It is used of the energizing *power* of love (Gal. 5.6); and of the *power* of prayer (James 5.16). It is used of the *effective working* of the word of God in those who believe (I Thess. 2.13). It is used of the control of God

in which he *works* all things according to his will (Eph.
1.11).

It is used of the death which *works* in Paul that the
Corinthians may have life (II Cor. 4.12). It is used of the
power of God which *wrought* in Christ in the Resurrection
(Eph. 1.20).

The word *energēma* occurs twice in the NT; it is used
twice in I Cor. 12.6, 10 of the varied gifts of those who
make up the Church, gifts which are set in being and in
motion by the power of God.

The word *energēs* is used three times in the NT. In I Cor.
16.9 it is used of the effective door of evangelization which
has opened to Paul. In Philemon 6 it is used of a fully
effective faith. In Heb. 4.12, where it is translated *powerful*,
it is used of the effectiveness of the word of God.

We must now go on to bring together the meaning of
the uses of this series of words in the NT.

The NT does not shirk or evade the fact that in this
world there is a power of evil in action (II Thess. 2.7, 9, 11;
Eph. 2.2; Rom. 7.5). The NT is not a speculative book, and
it does not stop to discuss and argue and debate the origin
and source of that power of evil; that power is there; and
the NT offers the greater power with which the evil power
can be defeated.

Let us remember that this whole group of words describes, not only power, but *effective power*, power which
achieves the aim and end and object which it set out
to achieve. Now it is to God that these words are mainly
applied; they therefore bear upon them the message of
the effectiveness of the power of God. Let us then see the
directions in which this power of God is effective.

(i) The power of God is *effective in the Resurrection*.
It was that power which wrought in Christ to raise him
from the dead (Eph. 1.19, 20; Col. 2.12). It is therefore true
that the *power of God is effective in the defeat of death*.
Not even man's last and final enemy can stand against the
power of God.

(ii) The power of God is *effective in the ministry*. God speaks through those who speak for him, and acts through those who act in his name (Eph. 3.7; Col. 1.29; Gal. 2.8). When a man enters the ministry, he not only thinks, he also listens for a voice; he not only brings to the task his own power, he is also clothed with the power of God.

(iii) The power of God is *effective within the Church*. The Church is built up and held together by the power of God (Eph. 4.16). Special gifts like the ministry of healing come from the power of God (Gal. 3.5); and all the differing gifts which are necessary for the administration and stewardship of the Church are supplied by the working of the power of God (I Cor. 12.6, 10, 11).

(iv) God's power is *effective in the defeat of sin*. Through Christ and in Christ there comes that power by which man's being of humiliation can be changed into Christ's being of glory (Phil. 3.21). The humiliations and the frustrations and the defeats of sin are swallowed up in the power of God.

(v) God's power is *effective in the world*. This is not a world which is out of control, but a world where God is working things out (Eph. 1.11). Behind the moving web of things there is design; the kaleidoscope of experience has a pattern, and the designer of the pattern is God.

(vi) God's power is *effective within*. It is not a power which coerces a man from outside; it is a power which floods a man's being from within (Eph. 3.20; Phil. 2.13). It is the power which makes a man most literally powerful.

(vii) There are certain ways and media through which God's power becomes effective.

(a) God's power becomes effective *through his word* (I Thess. 2.13; Heb. 4.12). The word is the source of power. Through God's word to men comes God's power for men. The Bible is not only a history-book; it is also a powerhouse.

(b) God's power becomes effective *through love* (Gal. 5.6). Love is the energizing power which turns knowledge into devotion and faith into sacrificial service. The power which comes to man is at one and the same time an indwelling and an out-going power.

(c) God's power becomes *effective through prayer* (James 5.16). Prayer is empowering contact with God. Prayer is not only a gateway to God for us; it is a channel for God to us.

(d) God's power becomes effective *through evangeliza-ition* (I Cor. 16.9). Man's evangelization of men becomes the channel of God's power to men.

(e) God's power becomes effective *through endurance* (II Cor. 1.6). The power of God does not come to the man who begins and gives up; it comes to the man who endures to the end.

The glory of the Christian life is that it is the life which is clothed with the *energeia*, the energy, the effective power of God himself.

ENTUGCHANEIN AND ENTEUXIS

PETITION TO THE KING

ENTUGCHANEIN, the verb, and *enteuxis*, the noun, are two of the prayer words of the NT. *Entugchanein* is usually translated *to make intercession for*.

In Rom. 8.26, 27 it is said that the Spirit *makes intercession for us*. In Rom. 8.34 Jesus is said to *make intercession for us*. In Rom. 11.2 Elijah is said *to make intercession* with God against Israel. In Heb. 7.25 it is said that Jesus ever lives *to make intercession for us*.

The noun *enteuxis* occurs twice in the NT. In I Tim. 2.1 it is translated *intercession*; and in I Tim. 4.5 it is translated *prayer*.

It is the idea which lies behind these words, the picture which they contain, which makes them so significant and so important.

Originally *entugchanein* meant quite simply *to meet a person*, to fall in with a person, to come close to a person. When we meet a person we talk to him and he talks to us; and so the word went on to mean *to converse with a person*; even further, it began to mean *to have intimate fellowship and communion with a person*.

For instance, when Socrates was near the end, and when he was preparing to die, he told his friends that he welcomed death because after death he would *have converse with* Palamedes and Ajax and others of the great men of the ancient days who died through unjust judgment (Plato, *Apology* 41b). To Socrates the reward of death was intimate fellowship with the great and good who had gone before.

Here then is the first idea in *entugchanein*. It speaks of the right to approach God; it speaks of the intimate fellowship which the Christian can enjoy with God; it means that we do not make our requests to God from a great distance and across some infinity of space, but that we can talk and converse with him as a man talks with his friend. As we meet our friends, so we can meet God.

But the word develops still another meaning. It begins by meaning simply to meet a person; it goes on to mean to have intimate converse and fellowship with a person; but finally it becomes in the papyri an almost technical word for *presenting a petition* to someone in authority and especially to the king.

Enteuxis, which originally meant simply a *meeting*, comes to be the usual word for a *petition* presented to the king.

There is an interesting papyrus which tells of twins, Thaues and Taous, who served in the Temple of Serapis at Memphis. They felt that they were being unjustly treated and that they were not receiving the treatment which they had been promised. Ptolemy Philometor and his queen, Cleopatra the Second, came on a visit to the temple, and the twins seized the opportunity to present the king with an *enteuxis,* a petition, which set out their grievances and which appealed for justice.

Enteuxis, then is the technical word for *a petition to a king;* and *entugchanein* is the technical word for presenting such a petition.

Here then is a tremendous picture. When we pray we are in the position of those who have undisputed access that they may bring their petitions to the king. When we pray it is to a king we come. Therein is set forth at once both the tremendous privilege of prayer, and the tremendous power of prayer.

We have the privilege of entry to the presence of the King of kings; and when we enter there we have all his power and greatness on which we may draw. Prayer is nothing less than entering into the presence of the Almighty and receiving the resources of the Eternal.

EPAGGELIA AND EPAGGELLESTHAI

THE WORDS OF PROMISE

IN the NT the noun *epaggelia* means a *promise,* and the verb *epaggellesthai* means to *promise.* We must begin by looking at the classical usage of these words, because in the case of these words the classical usages have very definite light to shed on the meaning and the flavour of these words in the NT.

(i) These words in classical Greek are very common—in fact they are almost technical—in connexion with *public announcements.* They are the words which are used of the announcement of the public games, or of the public sacrifices to the gods. They are used of announcements which are everybody's concern.

(ii) In classical Greek there is more than one word for a

promise, and the most interesting and significant thing about *epaggelia* is that its characteristic meaning is *a promise which is freely offered and volunteered*. It is not a promise which is extracted or coerced or wrung from someone.

It is not even a promise which is made on mutual approach and mutual agreement; that is *hyposchesis*. *Epaggelia* is characteristically a promise freely made and freely given. It has in it far more of a free offer than a conditioned promise.

(iii) In classical Greek *epaggelia* and *epaggellesthai* sometimes bear a meaning which has a tinge of fault in it. Sometimes they imply a profession, and a profession which is not met and carried out in actual practice. The words sometimes have to do with political canvassing.

They describe the manifesto of a candidate for office with all the promises of what he proposes to do, if he is elected to office, promises which are made rather as baits to the electorate than with any honest intention of fulfilling them.

The words sometimes have to do with the offers which the Sophists made. The Sophists were Greek teachers who arose in the fifth century B.C. and who offered to teach anybody anything for pay. The great teachers, like Plato and Isocrates, regarded these Sophists with intense dislike. They believed that all they did was to make people able to argue cleverly, until they could make the worse appear the better reason, and that they were out mainly for money.

They *professed* (*epaggellesthai*) to teach virtue, but it was an empty profession. They competed among themselves, each one *professing* to be able to give a better and more effective curriculum than his rival.

The words sometimes are used to describe a lover's professions. In the first flush of glamour and excitement of love, the lover will promise anything, but when it comes to actual performance, the professions are seen to be empty words. So the words can be used of a promise which is magnificently given, but meanly carried out.

Finally in regard to this usage, the words can be used of claims made for the curative properties of drugs. They are the words which would be used for the claims of patent medicines which profess to be panaceas for all diseases. Sometimes, then, these words can be used in connexion with a profession which is not backed by deeds to fit it.

In the NT the words *epaggelia* and *epaggellesthai* are uniformly and consistently of God's promises. There are, in fact, only two instances where they are used definitely of human promises.

In Acts 23.21 the Jews await the *promise* of the military commander of Jerusalem to send Paul down to Caesarea, in order that they may take steps to assassinate him on the way. In Mark 14.11 we read of the *promise* of the Jewish authorities to pay Judas the reward for information which will lead to the convenient arrest of Jesus.

But, apart from these two instances the words in the NT are always used of the divine promises and it is to these promises that we must proceed to turn our attention.

When we study the words of promise, we find that the promise did not start with the NT.

(i) God's promise was given specially to *the nation of Israel* (Rom. 9.4; Eph. 2.12). God offered Israel a unique position among the nations; in a special sense Israel was his peculiar people. The tragedy of Israel was that she misunderstood her function. She conceived of herself as having been promised special honour and privilege, when in point of fact she had been offered special duty and responsibility. God's offer is always the offer of a task to do for him.

(ii) God's promise to the nation of Israel derived specially from *Abraham*. The promise to Abraham was threefold. (a) It was the promise of the Promised Land (Acts 7.5; Heb. 11.9, 13). (b) It was the promise to Sara of a son, when the coming of a son seemed impossible (Rom. 9.9; Gal. 4.23, 28). (c) It was the promise that in him all nations of the earth would be blessed (Rom. 4.13; Gal. 3.16; Heb. 6.13).

Abraham was the man who was chosen that through him blessedness might come to the world. God chose Abraham as a man through whom he might act on men. God is always seeking men through whom he may act.

(iii) God's promise was the promise of a *Messiah* of the line of David (Acts 13.23, 32). The word *Messiah* and the word *Christ* are the same word. *Messiah* is the Hebrew and *Christ* is the Greek for *the anointed one*. God's promise was the promise of a King, through whom the kingdoms of the world would become the Kingdom of the Lord.

(iv) All the OT promises of God find their *fulfilment in Jesus Christ* (Rom. 15.8; II Cor. 1.20; Gal. 3.19, 29). When Jesus came, it was as if God said to men: 'Here is the one in whom all my promises come true.' Jesus is the one in whom there meet the dream of God and the dream of men.

(v) In Jesus there comes to men not only the fulfilment of the old promises; there come also even *better promises* (Heb. 8.6; 9.15). Jesus is not only the consummation and the hopes and the dreams of the past; he brings to men things more precious and things greater than ever they had dreamed of.

This is important, because it means that Jesus does not only fulfil the OT prophecies and ideals; he surpasses them. He brings into life, not only something which grew out of the past, but also something which is completely new.

When we see how far back the promise of God goes, it makes sense of history. We may promise a child some gift or some privilege with the intention of giving it to him when he is fit to use it and enjoy it and to enter into it. For instance, a father might plan and save in order to give a child the benefit of a university education, when the child came of age to benefit from such an education; and during the period of waiting, the father would do everything he could to train the child to reach a stage when he could be fit to enjoy the promise. That is what God did with men.

He chose a man; and chose a nation; that out of that nation there might come his Son in due time. Nor, in the choice of a nation, did God leave the rest of the world alone. Clement of Alexandria saw in pagan philosophy that which prepared the heathen for accepting Christ, just as much as the Law prepared the Jews. When we think of it this way we see the whole of history as a preparation of men to accept the promise and the offer of God.

Let us now see what God did promise to his people in Jesus Christ.

(i) God promised men *the gift of the Holy Spirit* (Luke 24.29; Acts 1.4; 2.23; Eph. 1.15). The Holy Spirit may be taken to be God active in the lives and in the minds of men. The Holy Spirit is the power and the presence and the person who guides men into strength and adequacy of life, power and clarity of thought, lucidity and persuasiveness of speech. The promise of the Spirit is the promise of God to make us live and think with his own power.

(ii) With the gift of the Spirit, God promised the gift of *forgiveness* (Acts 2.39). It is never enough to think of forgiveness as simply the remission of some penalty which should have fallen upon us. Forgiveness is essentially *the restoration of a lost relationship*. It was not that God was estranged from men; it was that men were estranged from God. Through that which Jesus Christ has done men can become friends with God.

(iii) God promises men *eternal life*, life in time and life in eternity (I Tim. 4.8; Titus 1.2; II Tim. 1.1; James 1.12; I John 2.25). Eternal life is not simply life which goes on for ever. It is true that the NT never forgets that God promised men the resurrection from the dead (Acts 26.6). But the essential of eternal life is not simply duration; it is quality.

It is told that once a drooping and depressed soldier came to Julius Caesar with a request to be allowed to commit suicide and so to end his life. Caesar looked at the dispirited figure: 'Man,' he said, 'were you ever really alive?'

Eternal life is something which can start here and now. Eternal life is the injection into the realm of time of something of the realm of eternity; it is the coming into human life of something of the life of God himself. It is the promise of God that if a man chooses to live life with Jesus Christ, heaven begins on earth. Into man's trouble and frustration there come the peace and power of God.

(iv) God promises the *Kingdom* to those who love him (James 2.5). It is too often the case that men think of the call of God as a call to a grim life in which all they wish for has to be given up, and all that is stern and hard has to be accepted. It is true that there is submission and discipline in the Christian life; but the end of the submission and the discipline is a kingdom, a royal power in life.

(v) God promises men *the coming again of his Son* (II Peter 3.4, 9). This simply means that God guarantees that there will be a consummation in history. The Stoics, who in NT times were the highest thinkers, conceived of history as circular. They said that, once every so many thousands of years, there was a conflagration which engulfed and destroyed all things, and that then the same old process began all over again. History was a treadmill, not a march to a goal.

When we divest the idea of the Second Coming of all the purely Jewish apparatus, and the purely temporary pictures, we are left with the one significant truth that in history there comes the consummation of the triumph of Christ.

(vi) God promises *rest for his people* (Heb. 4.1). Someone recently was asked what he thought was the greatest mark and characteristic of the modern world. His answer was: 'Tired eyes.'

Life is in any event a struggle; the Christian life takes all a man has to give. The NT describes it as a battle, a campaign, a race, an endurance test; but after it is ended there comes the rest of God; but rest is something which no man can enjoy unless he has done his best.

We must note still further *the nature of this promise* which is offered to the Christian.

(i) It is a *promise of God* (Luke 24.49; Acts 1.4). Here we find something which connects with one of the classical usages of these words. We saw, when we were studying the classical usage, that sometimes these words stood for a profession without a corresponding performance.

That is still so in the NT. I Tim. 2.10 urges Christian women to live a life which befits the faith which they profess. I Tim. 6.20, 21 speaks of the vain and empty knowledge which the intellectuals of the world profess. II Peter 2.19 speaks of those who make an illusory offer of liberty while they themselves are slaves to corruption. The NT more than once goes out of its way to stress the fact that God's promises, God's professions are true and dependable. God's promises are true for two reasons.

(a) They are true because God is *faithful*. 'He is faithful that promised' (Heb. 10.23). God cannot lie (Titus 1.2). God even guaranteed the promises by swearing by himself (Heb. 6.17). The promises of God are guaranteed by the truth of God.

(b) They are true because God is *powerful*. God is able to perform that which he has promised (Rom. 4.21). The promises of God are therefore guaranteed by the power of God. Men's promises may be empty professions, but God's promises are to be utterly relied on because God's truth cannot lie, and God's power cannot fail.

(ii) The promises of God are *founded on grace and not on law*. We already saw that *epaggelia* in classical Greek is a promise and an offer freely and voluntarily made. The promises of God are not dependent on man's merit or man's performance; they are dependent solely on the sheer generosity of God. God's promises were made, not because of man's virtue, but because of God's mercy. Behind them is not man's merit, but God's love.

(iii) The promises of God are therefore *to be appropriated by faith* (Rom. 4.14, 20; Gal. 3.24). They cannot be earned; they must be accepted. Man must rid himself of the pride which seeks to earn God's promises by works; he must have the humility which is ever content to be in God's debt, and which accepts God's promises in faith.

(iv) In spite of that the promises of God are *the motive of man's amendment*. It is because they have the promises that men must cleanse themselves (II Cor. 7.1). No man, who is in love, and whose love is answered, ever believed himself to be worthy of being loved. Any man who is loved well knows that he must spend all his life seeking to deserve the love which he can never deserve. It is so with us and God; we can never earn the promises of God, because they are given to us in the generosity of his love, but, nonetheless, we are under the life-long obligation to spend all our lives *trying* to deserve that love.

So this finally brings us to the things we must bring fully to enjoy the promises of God.

(i) We must bring *patience*. It was through patience that Jesus himself earned the promise, and the same must be true of us (Heb. 6.12, 15). We have to run and not be weary; we have to endure to the end; we have to learn to wait. It is patience—the ability to bear things—which in the end inherits and obtains the promise.

(ii) We must bring *loyalty*. It was through their utter fidelity, their unshakable loyalty, that the martyrs obtained the promises (Heb. 11.33). It is the man who is faithful unto death who obtains the crown.

(iii) We must bring *obedience*. It is after we have done the will of God that we receive the promise (Heb. 10.36). As in so many things, so in this, the gifts of God are given, but they are not given away. The promises of God are freely offered in the generosity of God. It is in patience, in loyalty, and in obedience that we shall most fully enter into them.

EPITAGĒ

THE ROYAL COMMAND

I N the NT, the word *epitagē* is peculiar to the writings of
Paul, if we include the Pastoral Epistles in the Pauline
writings. Paul makes two uses of this word.

(i) There are four passages where he uses it in connexion
with the message, the instruction and the advice which
he is giving. In I Cor. 7.6, where he is talking about certain
problems and customs in the married life, he contrasts that
which is by *permission* and that which is by *epitagē*. He
contrasts, as it were, that which is a human opinion and
that which is a direct, revealed command from God. He
contrasts that which is a piece of practical advice and that
which is a counsel of God and, therefore, a counsel of
perfection.

In 1 Cor. 7.25 he says that concerning virgins he has
no *epitagē*. Again, anything which he says is his own
opinion, and is not to be regarded as a definite divine command. He uses the same way of speaking in II Cor. 8.8.
When he is writing to Titus, he orders Titus to speak,
exhort, and rebuke with all *epitagē*, with the full authority
of the divine voice of God.

(ii) There are three passages where he uses it of the
direct action of God. In Rom. 16.26 he speaks of the
manifestation of Christ to the Gentiles as being in accord-
ance with the *epitagē*, the divine command, of God. In
Titus 1.3 he declares that the word which he preaches is
committed to him by the *epitagē* of God. In I Tim. 1.1 he
declares that he is an apostle by the *epitagē* of God.

In secular Greek, *epitagē* is used of the decrees of the
law. Diodorus Siculus (1.70) has an interesting passage on
the life of the kings of Egypt; 'The life which the kings of
the Egyptians lived was not like that of other men who

enjoy autocratic power, and do in all matters exactly as they please without being held to account, but all their acts are regulated by the *prescriptions* (*epitagai*) set forth in the law.' Clearly an *epitagē* is something which comes from and speaks with an authority than which none could be higher.

It is here that we have to add the evidence of the Septuagint. In the Septuagint the word *epitagē* occurs five times. In three instances it is used of a *royal command*. In Esth. 1.8 it is used of the *royal command* of Ahasuerus. In Dan. 3.16 Shadrach, Meshach and Abednego deny that they are answerable to the *epitagē, the royal command*, of Nebuchadnezzar which orders them to worship the image of the king.

In Wisdom 14.16, when the time of national degeneration is being described, it is said: 'By *the commandments* (*epitagai*) of princes the graven images received worship.' In the other two instances the word is connected with God.

In Wisdom 18.16 the sword of the word is *the unfeigned commandment* (*epitagē*) of God. In Wisdom 19.6 it is said that every part of the new creation will minister to *the several commandments* (*epitagai*) of God.

Clearly, then, this word *epitagē* has in it all the majesty of divine command.

But it is in the Greek of the papyri that the word gains its characteristic sense. There it is used for an order or an injunction, but especially for a divine command. Isias dedicates an altar to the mother of the gods, according to the *epitagē, the commandment*, of Cybele, which has come to him direct in a dream. Varius Pollio erects a pillar to the honour of the gods in obedience to the *epitagē, the command*, of God. *Epitagē* becomes the word of the divine command.

Here then are two great truths.

(i) The preacher's message is a divine command. When he is really preaching, he is speaking for God. He is bringing to men, not his own opinions, but the direct commands of God.

(ii) The preacher's commission is from God. Paul was supremely conscious that his task as a missionary to the Gentiles, his office as an apostle to the Church, came to him by the royal command, the *epitagē*, of God.

Paul has another way of saying that. Often he speaks of himself as an apostle by the *thelēma, the will*, of God. (I Cor. 1.1; II Cor. 1.1; Eph. 1.1; Col. 1.1) He speaks of himself as separated by God for his task from his mother's womb (Gal. 1.15). He speaks of necessity being laid upon him to preach (I Cor. 9.16). Paul always felt, not that he had chosen Christ, but that Christ had chosen him. He always thought of himself as a man who held the King's commission. For Paul, the ministry was not a profession; it was a vocation. It was not a trade; it was a calling. He came to it, not because he had chosen it as a career, but because God had chosen and called him to it.

Robert Robinson, the great Cambridge Baptist minister, had an experience of conversion. After it there were many who wished him to enter the ministry of the Church. He said: 'Lord, accomplish Thy will in all I have to say. *But God forbid that I should run before I am sent*.' The word *epitagē* enshrines the fact that no man may dare to contemplate the work of the ministry unless he is truly aware that he has received the King's commission to it.

EUSEBEIA

THE WORD OF TRUE RELIGION

THERE is a very great group of Greek words which is characteristic of the language of the Pastoral Epistles. As we shall see, they are not easy to translate, but they all have in them one essential idea.

There is *eusebeia*, the noun, which is usually translated *godliness*, in the AV. The ARSV usually retains this translation. Moffatt translates it either *piety*, or *religion*, in the sense of *true religion*.

There is *eusebēs*, the adjective, which the AV translates *devout* or *godly*, a translation which the ARSV retains; Moffatt translates it *religious, religiously-minded, or pious*.

There is *eusebein*, the verb, which means *to worship, to carry out the duties of true religion*. There is *eusebōs*, the adverb, which the AV translates *godly*.

There is the closely related word *theosebeia*, which the AV translates godliness, and the adjective *theosebēs*, which means *worshipping God*.

It can be seen that all these words come from the same root; and the root meaning of them all is *awe* in the presence of that which is more than human, *reverence* in the presence of that which is majestic and divine; not only do they express that feeling of awe and reverence, but they also imply a *worship* which befits that awe, and a life of active *obedience* which befits that reverence. The fact is that in so far as Greek has a word for *religion* that word is *eusebeia*.

Let us then begin by seeing what the Greeks themselves said about these words. The Platonic Definitions define *eusebeia* as *right conduct in regard to the gods*. The Stoics defined it *as knowledge of how God should be worshipped*.

Lucian (*De Calum.*) said that the man who is *eusebes*, pious, religious, is a *lover of the gods* (*philotheos*). Xenophon (*Memorabilia* 4.3.2) said that such a man was *wise concerning the gods*.

It was always the Greek custom to define every virtue and every good quality as the mean between two extremes. Virtue was the right point, the happy medium, between some defect and some excess.

So Plutarch says that *eusebeia* is the mean between *atheotēs*, which is *atheism*, and *deisidaimonia*, which is *superstition*; Philo said it was the mean between *asebeia*, which is *impiety*, and *deisidaimonia*.

That is to say, *eusebeia* is the right attitude to God and

to things divine, the attitude which does not eliminate God altogether, and which does not degenerate into futile superstition, the attitude which gives God the place he ought to occupy in life and in thought and in devotion.

Josephus sets *eusebeia* over against *eidōlolatreia*, which is *idolatry*. *Eusebeia* gives God *the right place*, and worships God in *the right way*. Plato urges all men to *eusebeia*, that we may avoid evil and obtain good, and so become the friends of God (Plato, *Symposium* 193d).

But not only does *eusebeia* put a man into the right relationship with God; it also puts him into the right relationship with men. Plato speaks of *eusebeia* both to God and to parents (Plato, *Republic* 615c).

In Greek thought the word *eusebeia* has certain uses which will still further illustrate the idea behind it. Even in pagan religion *eusebeia* was a word of a noble lineage.

(i) Sometimes it can mean that respect for the gods which issues in a careful carrying out of all the ritual which the worship of the gods demands. That is to say, sometimes it can be a word of correct ritual rather than of moral quality. There is an inscription in which the town of Priēnē is praised for its '*reverence for things divine*', that is for the care of the ritual of the temples of the gods. Payments to the temples are said to be *ex eusebeias, in consequence of piety*. This is to some extent the lower and the ritual meaning of the word.

(ii) Sometimes the word can mean *loyalty*, but that loyalty is always to a royal figure. In the papyri there is a letter in which the Emperor Claudius, after a visit to Britain, writes to thank a certain club for a golden crown, which they had presented to him, and which he regards as a token of their *eusebeia*, their *loyalty*. Nero invites the Greeks to meet him at Corinth in order that he may requite them for their good will and *eusebeia, loyalty*, to him. So then *eusebeia* can express a man's loyalty to his king.

(iii) But the word goes higher than that. To Sophocles *eusebeia* was the greatest of all the virtues. Heracles advises Philoctetes 'to have respect for what is due to heaven' (eusebein). He goes on to say that everything else stands second to this in the counsels of Zeus; that eusebeia goes beyond death with a man, and is the virtue which can never perish (Sophocles, *Philoctetes* 1440-1444). To him eusebeia was the foundation stone of all virtue. Maybe the best of all definitions of eusebeia is in the passage of Xenophon's *Memorabilia* (4.8.11) in which he pays his final tribute to the memory of Socrates: 'For myself I have described him as he was; so religious (eusebēs) that he did nothing without counsel from the gods; so just that he did no injury, however small, to any man, but conferred the greatest benefits on all who dealt with him; so self-controlled that he never chose the pleasanter rather than the better course. So wise that he was unerring in his judgment of the better and the worse, and needed no counsellor, but relied on himself for his knowledge of them; masterly in expounding and defining such things; no less masterly in putting others to the test, and convincing them of error and exhorting them to follow virtue and gentleness. To me then he seemed to be all that a truly good and happy man must be.' That is the description of what the Greek regarded as eusebeia, true religion, and none can say that it is not a noble conception.

From the Greek point of view, we may note one final fact. The Greeks used eusebeia to translate the equally noble Latin word pietas. *Pietas* was *the spirit of devotion to goodness, to honour, to honesty and to duty.*

Warde Fowler has written: 'The quality known to the Romans as *pietas* rises, in spite of trial and danger, superior to the enticements of individual passion and selfish ease. Aeneas's *pietas* became a sense of duty to the will of the gods, as well as to his father, his son, his people; and this duty never leaves him.'

All the nobility of pagan ethics at their best was in this word eusebeia before the Christian faith annexed it and made it even greater.

Now we must turn to the biblical use of *eusebeia*. In the Septuagint *eusebeia* is not common; but there are two occurrences of it which are very illuminating. In Isa. 11.2 *eusebeia* is used for *the fear of the Lord*, which is one of the gifts of the Spirit; and in Prov. 1.7 it is used for that *fear of the Lord* which is the beginning of wisdom. Here again we see that basically *eusebeia* is the right attitude to God, the attitude of awe, of reverence, of worship and of obedience.

But there is one book written between the Old and New Testaments which is dominated through and through by the idea of *eusebeia*; that is Fourth Maccabees.

That book was written sometime in the first century B.C. It was written in a time of trouble for the Jews, and it was written by a Pharisee who above all things loved the Law. He saw that the one necessity of life was to master the passions, and the one way to master the passions was to obey the Law; and to him that mastery and that obedience were *eusebeia*. Those who with their whole heart give heed to *piety* (*eusebeia*) alone are able to overcome the passions of the flesh, in the faith that like our patriarchs, Abraham, Isaac and Jacob, we are not dead to God, but live to God. For is it actually possible that anyone who philosophizes *piously* (*eusebōs*) according to the complete rule of philosophy (i.e. the Law), who believes also in God, and who knows that it is blessedness to endure any affliction on behalf of virtue, will not get mastery over his passions by his *piety* (*eusebeia*)? (IV Mac. 7.18-22).

The writer of that book says that the Jewish philosophy, that is, the Law, 'instructs us in *godliness* (*eusebeia*) so that we may worship the only living God in a manner befitting his majesty' (IV Mac. 5.24). Still again we have this basic conception that *eusebeia* essentially means to give God the place he ought to possess in our minds, in our hearts and in our lives.

Now we turn to the NT itself. *Eusebeia* occurs once in Acts. In Acts 3.12 Peter and John protest that they have not

healed the lame man at the Temple gate by their own
power or *eusebeia* (AV, *holiness*; Moffatt and ARSV, *piety*).

Eusebeia occurs ten times in the Pastorals. In I Tim. 2.2
it is the aim of the Christian life that we should live in all
godliness (Moffatt, *piety*) and honesty. In I Tim. 3.16 it is
said: Great is the mystery of *eusebeia* (AV, *godliness*;
Moffatt: Great is the divine truth of our *religion*; ARSV:
Great is the mystery of our *religion*).

In I Tim. 4.7 the Christian is bidden to exercise himself
unto *godliness* (ARSV retains *godliness*; Moffatt translates:
Train for the *religious life*). In I Tim. 4.8 *eusebeia* is said to
be profitable for all things (AV and ARSV, *godliness*;
Moffatt, *religion*).

In I Tim. 6.3 there is the doctrine which is according to
eusebeia (AV and ARSV, *godliness*; Moffatt, *piety*). In I
Tim. 6.5, 6, those who seek to make money out of *eusebeia*
are condemned, but it is pointed out that *eusebeia* with
contentment is great gain (AV and ARSV, *godliness*; Moffatt,
religion).

In I Tim. 6.11 the Christian is bidden to follow after
eusebeia (AV and ARSV, *godliness*; Moffatt, *piety*). II Tim.
3.5 speaks of those who have only an outward form of
eusebeia (AV, *godliness*; Moffatt and ARSV, *religion*). Titus
1.1 speaks of truth which is according to *eusebeia* (AV and
ARSV, *godliness*; Moffatt, *the religious life*).

Outside the Pastorals *eusebeia* occurs four times in
Second Peter. II Peter 1.3 speaks of life according to
eusebeia (AV and ARSV, *godliness*; Moffatt, *piety*). II Peter
1.6, 7 bids the Christian to add *eusebeia* to patience, and
brotherly love to *eusebeia* (AV and ARSV, *godliness*;
Moffatt, *piety*).

In II Peter 3.11 there is the phrase, All holy conversation
and *eusebeia* (AV and ARSV, *godliness*; Moffatt, What holy
and *pious* men you ought to be).

Before we can make a pattern of the meaning of *eusebeia*
we must look at the use of its kindred words in the NT.
But we can already see that *eusebeia* means true *godliness*,

true *piety*. We can see that in fact *eusebeia* is the word for true *religion*. There is therefore no word whose meaning it is more necessary fully to understand.

In the NT the adjective *eusebēs* occurs four times. In Acts 10.2 Cornelius is *eusebēs* and one who fears the Lord (AV and ARSV, *devout*; Moffatt, *religious*). In Acts 10.7 we read that Cornelius sent a soldier who was *eusebēs* as his messenger to Peter (AV and ARSV, *devout*; Moffatt, *religiously minded*). In II Peter 2.9 it is said that God delivers those who are *eusebēs* out of temptation (AV and ARSV, *godly*; Moffatt, *pious folk*). This word does not occur often but once again we see that the basic idea is a right and reverent attitude to God.

The adverb *eusebōs* occurs twice. In II Tim. 3.12 the warning is given that all who live *eusebōs* will be persecuted (AV, *godly*). The AV uses *godly* both as an adjective and as an adverb. (As an adverb, as here, more correctly, but unpronounceably, it would be *godlily*. ARSV, all who *live a godly life*; Moffatt, all who *live the religious life*.) Titus 2.12 uses the same phrase, to live *eusebōs* (AV, to live *godly*; ARSV, *to live godly lives*; Moffatt, to live a *life of piety*).

The verb *eusebein* occurs twice. In Acts 17.23 Paul uses it when he speaks to the Athenians of that which they ignorantly *worship*. In I Tim. 5.4 the children of widows are told that they must *show piety* at home, by paying their debt to their parents. The ARSV translates this: Let them first learn *their religious duty* to their own family. Moffatt translates it: Let them learn that *the first duty of religion* is to their own household. When we come to make the Christian pattern of true religion we shall see that this saying must be given a very prominent place in it.

To complete this study we must take in two kindred words. In the NT the word *theosebeia* occurs once. The difference between *eusebeia* and *theosebeia* is this. It is the *seb-* part of the word which means *reverence* or *worship*. *Eu* is the Greek word for *well*; therefore, *eusebeia* is worship, reverence well and rightly given. *Eusebeia* stresses the rightness of the reverence, its freedom from superstitions and imperfections and improprieties.

Theos is the Greek word for *God*; therefore, *theosebeia* means literally *the worship of God*. *Theosebeia* is therefore the wider word, but in effect the two words mean almost the same, except that *eusebeia* emphasizes the rightness of the worship.

The one instance of *theosebeia* is in I Tim. 2.10 where advice is given to women who profess *theosebeia* (AV, professing *godliness*; ARSV, who profess *religion*; Moffatt, who *make a religious profession*).

In the NT the adjective *theosebēs* occurs once, in John 9.31. God hears the prayers of the man who is *theosebēs* (AV and ARSV, *a worshipper of God*; Moffatt, anyone who is *devout*).

We have now studied in full the occurrences of these great words in the NT. We have seen that the basic meaning which lies behind them is the right attitude to God and to the holiness, the majesty and the love of God. It now remains to work out what that right attitude is.

(i) *Eusebeia*, true religion, comes through the divine power of Jesus Christ (II Peter 1.3). Without the vision of Jesus, without the help of Jesus, without the presence of Jesus true religion is impossible. I Tim. 3.16 speaks, as the AV has it, about 'the mystery of godliness'. In the NT and in the ancient world a *mystery* was not something which was mysterious in the sense of being hard to understand. A mystery was something which was unintelligible to the uninitiated, but crystal clear to those who had been initiated and who had learned to understand. A mystery was a divine secret, unintelligible to the outsider, but open and precious to the true worshipper. So Jesus brought to men the secret of true religion. In him men both see God and learn how to worship God.

(ii) But although *eusebeia*, true religion, is the gift of the power of Jesus Christ, it is none the less something which a man must struggle and battle to attain. We must *train* ourselves to religion (I Tim. 4.7). We must *follow after* religion (I Tim. 6.11).

The first word that Paul uses (*gumnazein*) is an *athlete's* word; and the second passage comes exactly and immediately before he bids Timothy fight the good fight; it is the *soldier's* word. The Christian is at once the *athlete* and the *soldier*. As the athlete trains himself for the contest so the Christian must train himself to be the follower of Christ. As the soldier must battle towards final victory, so the Christian must dauntlessly and tirelessly face the struggle of goodness.

(iii) This gift and this struggle combined bring three things. (a) *Eusebeia* brings *trouble*. The man who will live for Christ must expect to receive persecution (II Tim. 3.12). To be different from the world, to have a different set of standards and a different set of aims, is always a perilous thing. It is not peace but glory that Christ offers us.

(b) *Eusebeia* brings *power*. It was *holiness* and *power* combined that the Jerusalem crowds saw in Peter and John (Acts 3.12). Christ never sends a man a task without also sending him the power to do it. In a world of collapse the Christian alone has the power to stand foursquare against the assaults of all that time can do.

(c) *Eusebeia* brings *God*. For the true worshipper of God the way is ever open to God (John 9.31). In every time of trial the Christian can retire to the presence of God to emerge with a power that is not his own power. The Christian has continual access to and contact with the power of the Eternal.

(iv) *Eusebeia* is the mark of the Christian life. The aim of the Christian, and the duty of the Christian, is to live with godliness and honesty (I Tim. 2.2). 'A saint', as someone has said, 'is someone who makes it easier to believe in God.' Even within the world something of heaven's grace and glory cling to the life of the Christian. He too brings God to men.

(v) *Eusebeia* is the origin of all true theology and of all true thinking (I Tim. 6.3; Titus 1.1). One of the great neglected truths of the Christian life is that inspiration and revelation are morally conditioned. God can only tell a man what that man is capable of receiving and understanding. The closer a man lives to God, the more God can say to him. The great thinker must first of all be a good man. To learn about God we must first of all obey God. It may well be true that the man who says that he cannot understand the Christian faith does not want to understand it, and may even be afraid to understand it.

(vi) *Eusebeia* must never be confounded with material prosperity. The man who sees in his religion, or who uses his religion as, the way to material success has a debased view of what religion is (I Tim. 6.5). But true religion is the way to the real profit and the real joy in this world and in the world to come (I Tim. 4.8). The essence of this matter lies in the basic truth that true happiness never results from the possession of things. It is not in things to give either satisfaction or peace. True happiness lies entirely in personal relationships. If a man has love he has everything. And the greatest of all personal relationships is the relationship with God. If that relationship is right, then life is true happiness.

(vii) *Eusebeia* is the product of the life which is lived in the light of eternity. In II Peter 3.11, holy conversation and godliness are urged upon men, because Christ comes again. It may be that to-day, after the long slow centuries have passed, we have not so keen an expectation of the Second Coming as the early Church had. But, at the same time, it remains true for every man that no man knows when he must leave time to begin on eternity. And true religion is characteristic of the man whose life is such that he is ever in readiness for the summons of God.

(viii) For all that, true *eusebeia* does not separate a man from his fellow men. To his *eusebeia*, as an essential part of it, he must add *brotherly love* (II Peter 1.6, 7). True religion looks both to God and to man.

There is a religion which separates a man from his fellow men. It may make him, as it made the monks and the hermits, decide to leave the life of the world for the life of contemplation and meditation and prayer. But prayer and contemplation and meditation, great and essential as they are, are imperfect and truncated and even unchristian, if they do not result in action. It is true that there are times when a Christian must retire from the world, but he only retires that he may return better able to face the world, to help the world, and to live with his fellow men. The Christian does not live with God to avoid his fellow men, but rather to be able better to solve the problem of living together.

(ix) *Eusebeia*, true religion, is not confined to the precincts of the church, and is not limited to the worship and the liturgy and the ritual of the church. True religion begins at home. Those who would be real servants of Christ and of his Church must remember that *the first duty of religion is to their own household* (I Tim. 5.4). If a man or a woman's church work involves the neglect of his or her own family then it is irreligion, not religion.

There can never be a Christian church which is not founded on the Christian home; and the most important religious work is not the work that is done in the public, but the work that is done in the privacy of the home, and amidst what ought to be the circle of those most dear.

Jesus said that where two or three are gathered together he is there in the midst of them (Matt. 18.20); and it has been suggested that the two or three are father, mother and child. Whether or not that be so, it is certainly true that true Christianity, like true charity, must begin at home, even if it is also true that it cannot stay there but must go out to the wider sphere of the Church and of the world.

When the Christian thinkers took over the word *eusebeia* it was already a great word, but they filled it with a content

which made it far greater than ever it could be on the lips
of any pagan thinker.

HUBRIS, HUBRIZEIN, HUBRISTĒS

THE WORDS OF IMPIOUS PRIDE

T H E words *hubris, hubrizein* and *hubristēs* do not occur
often in the NT, but they are words which are well worth
studying, because to the Greeks these were the words which
were concerned with the supreme sin, which could not do
anything else but breed destruction and total ruin.

They are words which are not easy to translate. *Hubris* is
a noun which means *wanton insolence*: *hubristēs* is also a
noun and means *one who acts with wanton insolence*:
hubrizein is a verb which means *to treat with wanton insolence*. But the basic idea in all these words is *the pride
which erects itself against God and man alike*.

W. G. de Burgh writes of *hubris*: 'Its root meaning is
the violent over-stepping of the mark, the insolence of
triumph, and the pride of life that tramples underfoot the
unwritten laws of gods and men. *Hubris* is the closest Greek
equivalent for "sin". Its most characteristic application
was to the insatiable thirst for power which drives a man
or a nation headlong, as though possessed by a demon, on
the path of unbridled self-assertion. This blinding passion,
outraging alike personal liberty and public law, lures the
victim in a frenzy of self-confidence towards destruction.
It provokes *nemesis*, the feeling of righteous indignation,
in the gods and in his fellow men.'

Ernest Myers speaks of 'the sin of *hubris*, of insolence,
ready to trample in violence over law and liberty to gratify
selfish lust and pride'.

The basic evil of *hubris* is that when *hubris* enters into
a man's heart that man forgets that he is a creature and

that God is the Creator. *Hubris* is the sin whereby a man forgets his humanity and makes himself equal with God. *Hubris* is that insolent arrogance which forgets the essential creatureliness of the condition of being a man.

This was accentuated by the strange Greek conception of *the envy of the gods* (*phthonos theōn*). It was the strange conception of the Greeks that the gods grudged man all happiness, all prosperity and all success. That goes as far back as Homer. Even a fair reputation for kindliness and honour was a thing which the gods might grudge and envy men, for was Poseidon, the sea god, not jealous of the Phaeacians because 'they gave safe escort to all men' (Homer, *Odyssey* 8.566)?

The same conception of this envy of the gods is there in Pindar. When he sings in praise of Corinth, he adds the prayer to the sovereign Lord of Olympia not to allow his envy to be awakened by such word of praise (Pindar *Olymp.* 13.24). In the *Pythians* he prays that the family of the Aleuadae may continue to fare well. 'Of the happy things of Hellas they have received no small portion; I pray that they meet with no reverses from the envious gods' (Pindar, *Pyth.* 10.19). It is the same in the *Isthmians*: 'I will set a garland upon my hair and sing. But let not the envy of the immortal gods bring confusion on me' (Pindar, *Isth.* 7.39). The Greek was haunted by this idea of the envy of the gods.

It may be said that all early Greek history is written on the theme of the envy of the gods. Herodotus draws the picture of Xerxes planning to invade Greece, and of Artabanus seeking to restrain him from an ambition which is bound to awaken the envy of the gods: 'You see how God smites with his thunderbolts the tallest animals, and does not allow them to exalt themselves, whereas the smaller animals in no way provoke his wrath; you see how he ever hurls his shafts at the highest buildings and trees, for it is God's custom to cut down whatever exceeds in point of greatness. Thus a mighty host may be destroyed by a small one, when God, becoming envious, smites them with panic or with lightning, so that they perish in a manner unworthy of themselves. For God will not suffer any but himself to think high thoughts' (Herodotus, 7.10). In the same way Amasis addresses his warning letter to Polycrates: 'Your great successes do not please me, knowing as I do that the divine nature is jealous. I would prefer that I myself and those I care for should be successful in some things and unsuccessful in others, experiencing through life alternate good and evil fortune, rather than that they should invariably succeed. For I have never yet heard of anyone who was successful in everything, without perishing miserably, root and branch, at the last' (Herodotus, 3.40).

At the back of life for the Greek there was the terror of success, for success was bound to awaken the envy of the gods.

To be too successful, to have too much good fortune, to triumph too much, was to court disaster, for it was to incur the inevitable envy of the gods. 'Seek not to become Zeus' said Pindar. 'Mortal things befit a mortal' (Pindar, *Isth.* 5.14). 'If anyone shall possess wealth and shall excel others in beauty, and have won distinction by display of strength in the games, let him not forget that his raiment is on mortal limbs, and that the earth shall be his garment at the last' (Pindar, *Nem.* 11.13).

Even man's voyaging throughout the world must be circumscribed. At the end of the Mediterranean Sea there stood the Pillars of Hercules. Better for a man not to venture beyond. 'By their manly prowess they have touched the Pillars of Hercules, at the boundaries of the world. Beyond that I bid them seek for no further excellence' (Pindar, *Isth.* 4.11).

The same refrain runs through Aeschylus. The man upon a too prosperous voyage, in the midst of a calm sea, strikes a hidden reef, and the end is shipwreck (Aeschylus, *Aga-*

memnon 993). Xerxes is defeated with all his might and
the defeat is due to 'the envy of the gods' (Aeschylus,
Persae 365).

From beginning to end, classical literature is permeated with this fear of the envy of the gods; and this
conception that the supreme sin is the failure of a man to
remember that he is a man.

Now if all that be true—and to the Greek it was the
truest thing in the universe—then if success is dangerous,
pride in success is fatal. And *hubris* is this arrogant and
insolent pride which forgets the gods. 'Very certainly,' said
Aeschylus, 'insolence, *hubris*, is the child of godlessness'
(Aeschylus, *Eumenides* 533). 'Zeus,' he says, 'of a truth is
a chastiser of overweening pride and corrects with a heavy
hand. Therefore, now that my son has been warned to
prudence by the voice of God, do ye instruct him by
admonitions of reason, to cease from drawing on himself
the punishment of heaven by his vaunting rashness' (Aeschylus, *Persae* 827-831). Darius says of his son Xerxes
and his disastrous expedition against Greece: 'Mortal
though he was, he thought in his folly that he would gain
the mastery over all the gods' (*ibid.* 794).

The trouble about this pride is that it grows ever greater
as a man's life goes on: 'An ancient *hubris* ever breeds a
fresh and living *hubris* to add to human woes' (Aeschylus,
Agamemnon 760); and that is the very reason why 'from
good fortune there sprouts forth for posterity insatiate
calamity'.

Sophocles has it: '*Hubris* begets a tyrant' (Sophocles,
Oedipus Tyrannus 873). It is this overweening pride which
makes a tyrant and men and gods hate a tyrant. Euripides
has it: 'If you have more of good than evil, being a man,
you will do right well. But, dear child, refrain from evil
thoughts; cease from *hubris*, presumptuous pride; for to
wish to be greater than God is nothing other than *hubris*'
(Euripides, *Hippolytus* 472-474). To try to take one's own
way, to resist the will of the gods, to think one knows

better than the gods, is *hubris*, insolent, arrogant, over-weening pride.

This innate terror of *hubris* was burned into the consciousness of the Greek. For a man to be drunk with success, for a man to get the idea that he can direct life and that he can cope with life and that he can forge out unbroken success, for a man to forget God is *hubris*. For a nation to seek for world power and world dominion, and to map out vast schemes of conquest, leaving the gods entirely out of the reckoning, is *hubris*. For a philosopher to grasp a few natural laws and then to think that he can explain the universe and eliminate God is *hubris*. *Hubris* is there whenever a man forgets that he is a man, and forgets that God has the last word, and for the Greek that *hubris* was rendered doubly disastrous because of the envy of the gods.

So far we have been thinking of *hubris* in what might be called its theological sense in Greek thought. But these words have also an *ethical* sense. To put it in another way, if a man has *hubris* in his heart, that *hubris* will come out in a certain attitude to his fellow men, and a certain treatment of them. Just as there is a certain overweening pride in a man's attitude to God, so there can be a certain insolent arrogance in his attitude to his fellow men.

The Greek ethical writers regarded *hubris* as the greatest of sins towards one's fellow men; and in it they identified two basic elements.

(i) *Hubris* is the outcome of allowing the passions to rule. Plato has it: 'When opinion conquers, and, by the help of reason, leads us to the best, the conquering principle is called temperance (*sōphrosunē*); but when desire, which is devoid of reason, rules in us, and drags us to pleasure, that power of misrule is called *hubris*' (Plato, *Protagoras* 238a). The man who is governed by *hubris* is governed by passion and not reason. Aristotle draws a distinction between the temperate man (*sōphrōn*), whose conduct is governed by law, and the man who commits outrage (*hubrizein*). Such a man obeys the dictates of passion and not of law and reason.

(ii) But to the Greeks the really terrible thing about *hubris* was that it was partly the product of sheer contemptuous insolence, and partly the product of the sheer desire to hurt other people. *Hubris* is committed in contempt of others (Aristotle, *Nicomachean Ethics* 1149b 22). Speaking with deliberate attempt to insult and to give offence is *hubris* (*ibid.* 1125a 9). *Hubris* is that completely deliberate way of slighting a man, which is bound to beget anger (*ibid.* 1149a 32). *Hubris* is fundamentally a perverted and morbid thing (*ibid.* 1148b 30). But the most terrible thing about *hubris* was the pleasure it takes in inflicting injury. It is wanton insolence done simply for the pleasure it gives to see someone else suffer (*ibid.* 1149b 22).

The Greeks drew a clear distinction between three things. *Anger* is not deliberate; a man blazes into anger because he cannot help it. *Revenge* is taken with the clear intention of getting something back; vengeance is for the sake of retaliation. But *hubris*, wanton insolence, is the spirit which hurts someone in a cold, detached way, and then stands back to see the other person wince. It is hurting for hurting's sake, and it always involves deliberate humiliation of the person injured.

Aristotle describes it fully (*Rhetoric* 2.2.3); 'Insolence (*hubris*) is another form of slight, as being an act of injury or annoyance involving the disgrace of the sufferer, not for the sake of any benefit to the agent beyond the mere fact of its having been done, but only for his personal gratification; for the requital of injuries is not insolence (*hubris*), but revenge. The source of the pleasure found in insolent action is the feeling that in injuring others we are claiming an exceptional superiority to them.'

It can easily be seen that to the Greek *hubris* was the cruellest of all sins. It came from allowing the passions to overthrow the reason, as Plato saw it. Aristotle saw it in an even worse light. For him it came from sheer contempt.

The insolent man treated his fellow men as some one might squash, or tear the wings from, a fly. It came from the sheer delight in inflicting needless and useless pain. It came from sheer pleasure in seeing people wince, and knowing that their hearts had been wounded. It always aimed at the public humiliation of the person injured. It is wickedness at its most cruel.

These words acquired a certain almost standard usage in colloquial Greek contemporary with the NT, and that usage we must now go on to investigate.

In the contemporary colloquial Greek in the time of the NT, in the papyri, this group of words has a special flavour and a special connection. They are consistently used in connection with insulting, outrageous and humiliating conduct.

A man complains that he was *grossly insulted* (*hubrizein*) by a certain Apollodorus. A wife lays a complaint against her husband that he has consistently ill-treated and *insulted* her, and has had recourse even to physical violence. A man complains he has been bound, stripped naked and *mal-treated*. A man appeals to the emperor, who writes back: 'Your citizenship will in nowise be injured, nor will you be *subjected to corporal punishment*' (*hubrizein*).

The words consistently express insulting and outrageous treatment, and especially treatment which is calculated publicly to insult and openly to humiliate the person who suffers from it. One of the usages which best illustrates the whole flavour and tone of these words is the use in the Septuagint of II Sam. 10. The chapter tells how Hanun, king of Ammon, cut short the garments of King David's ambassadors, and shaved off half their beards, and then sent them back to their master. That treatment was *hubris*. It was insult, outrage, public humiliation all combined.

Now we turn to the NT usages of these words.

(i) In one case *hubris* is used simply of the disaster which will follow a sea voyage taken against the advice of Paul

(Acts 27.10, 21). In one case one of the scribes complains that Jesus has treated the scribes with insolence (*hubrizein*) in his denunciation of them (Luke 11.45).

(ii) The word *hubristēs*, a man of arrogant insolence, is once used to describe one of the characteristic sins of the pagan world (Rom. 1.30). There it describes the pride of godlessness.

(iii) Once Paul uses *hubristēs* to describe his own conduct toward the Church in the days when he was a persecutor (I Tim. 1.13). In those days Paul had taken a savage delight in seeing the Christians hurt and humiliated. Nothing could better show how savage a persecutor Paul once was.

(iv) *Hubrizein* is twice used of the treatment which Paul received at the hands of his persecutors on his missionary journeys. It is used of what happened to him at Iconium (Acts 14.5), and at Philippi (I Thess. 2.2). In the list of his sufferings in II Cor. 12.10 Paul includes the things he suffered from *hubris*. The Christian had to suffer not only cruelty but also public humiliation.

(v) Jesus uses the word *hubrizein* of the treatment which he himself knew he would suffer at Jerusalem (Luke 18.32). Jesus knew that the cruelty of men would leave nothing undone to hurt and to wound and to insult and to humiliate him.

(vi) But the most suggestive usage of all, the usage which gathers up the whole meaning of the words, is in Matt. 22.6. There the word *hubrizein* is used of the conduct of the people who ill-treated and killed the messengers of the king who brought the king's invitation to the king's feast. There we have the very essence of sin. God sends his invitation into the world, and men reject it; that is *hubris*. That is man erecting himself against God, man in his pride defying God, man forgetting that he is a creature and that God is Creator, man in arrogance turning his back on God. That is man deliberately hurting God, for sin is always the breaking of God's heart more than it is the breaking of God's law. That is man publicly humiliating God, for it is the most hurting and humiliating thing in the world to offer love only to have that love spurned and contemptuously refused.

Hubris is mingled pride and cruelty. *Hubris* is the pride which makes a man defy God, and the arrogant contempt which makes him trample on the hearts of his fellow men.

HUPERĒPHANIA
AND HUPERĒPHANOS

THE WORDS OF CONTEMPT

T H E words *huperēphania* and *huperēphanos* are not very common in the NT, but they describe one of the gravest and most basic sins in human nature. *Huperēphania* is a noun, and is usually translated *pride*. *Pride* is one of those sins which Jesus says proceeds out of a man's heart (Mark 7.22).

Huperēphanos is an adjective which means *proud, arrogant, over-weening*. In the Magnificat it is said that God has scattered the *proud* in the imagination of their hearts (Luke 1.51). The *proud* are included by Paul in his terrible list of this sinners of this world (Rom. 1.30). The *proud* are included among the sinners of the last days in II Tim. 3.2. Both James and Peter quote the saying of Prov. 3.34 that God gives grace to the humble but resists the *proud* (James 4.6; I Peter 5.5).

The sin of *huperēphania* was a sin which the ancient world knew well and about which its ethical teachers had much to say. They derived *huperēphanos* from two Greek words, *huper* which means *above*, and *phainesthai*, which means to *show oneself*. The man who was *huperēphanos* was *the man who showed himself above*.

It does not so much mean the man who is conspicuous

and to whom others look up, as the man who stands on his own little self-created pedestal and looks down. The characteristic of the man who is *huperēphanos* is that he looks down on everyone else, secure in his own arrogant self-conceit.

First of all let us look at the usage of these words in classical Greek. Xenophon uses the word to describe *the cruel insolence* of the character of a young king who does not know how to rule his people (Xenophon, *Cyropaedia* 5.2.27). The enemies of Socrates accused him of showing *lofty disdain* for his fellow men (Plato, *Symposium* 219c). Plato accuses Homer of depicting Achilles as displaying *overwhelming contempt* for gods and men (Plato, *Republic* 391c). The Greeks told how the new gods headed by Zeus drove the older gods from power, and Aeschylus speaks of the *overweening spirit* of Zeus towards the older gods (Aeschylus, *Prometheus* 405).

Theophrastus has one of his character studies which draws the picture of the man who is *huperēphanos*. He begins by defining *huperēphania* as the spirit of the man who has contempt for everyone except himself. The man who is *huperēphanos* will never pay the first visit to someone else. When he walks on the streets, he never talks to anyone whom he meets, but stalks by with bent head and averted eyes, too proud even to look at other people. When he is elected to office, he declines it, on the grounds that he is too busy to serve. If he gives an entertainment, he never sits down with his guests, but orders some underling to look after them. When he writes a letter, he never says: 'Would you do me the favour of doing such and such a thing?' He says: 'I want this done as quickly as possible.' (Theophrastus, *Characters* 24). The man who is *huperēphanos* has a contempt for everyone else.

As F. J. Hort has it: '*Huperēphania* is shown in overweening treatment of others. . . . It springs from a false view of what our relations with other persons are.' It flaunts its greatness in the face of men.

Plutarch, in his life of Pompey, describes how the pirates haunted the Mediterranean Sea, and made voyaging perilous for merchantmen, and how Pompey exterminated them. He says that in the days when the pirates held sway, they sailed in ships with gilded sails and purple awnings and silver oars, so that 'more annoying than the fear they inspired was the *flaunting extravagance* of their equipment'. Their very pride was an insult to men.

We can see already that *huperēphania* is an ugly sin; we must go on to look at it in two of its most characteristic manifestations.

(i) *Huperēphania* and wealth were apt to go hand in hand. Riches and possessions have a way of begetting arrogance and pride. Stobaeus preserves a fragment of a writer called Callicratides : 'It is inevitable that those who have great possessions should become inflated with pride; then that being inflated with pride they should become boastful (*alazōn*); then that being boastful they should become arrogant (*huperēphanos*), and think that there is no one like themselves' (Stobaeus, 85.15).

Aristotle, in his *Constitution of Athens* (5.3), quotes a saying of Solon, the great Greek lawgiver : 'Commonly the blame for trouble in a state attaches to the rich.' So at the very beginning of his elegy he said that he feared above all covetousness and *arrogance*, because enmity always arose because of them.

In his *Art of Rhetoric* (1390b 33) Aristotle returns to the same point : 'The characters which accompany wealth are plain for all to see. The wealthy are insolent and *arrogant*, being mentally affected by the acquisition of wealth, for they seem to think that they possess all good things; for wealth is a kind of standard of value of everything else, so that everything seems purchasable by it.'

In the papyri a letter speaks of a man who has come to *despise* his friends because he has grown wealthy. Another writer, writing to a former friend who has dropped him, says : 'You doubtless had better things to do; that was why you *neglected* us.' *Huperēphania* is the pride which comes from possessions; the arrogance of the man who is rich and who believes that his money can buy him anything; the insolent pride of the man who believes that every thing and every man has a price, and that he can pay it.

(ii) But *huperēphania* can go even further than that. *Huperēphania* can become the pride and arrogance which in the end despise God. The literature of the Jews between the Old and the New Testaments has much to say of this word and this characteristic. '*Huperēphania* is hateful before God and men. . . . The beginning of *huperēphania* is when a man departs from the Lord, and when his heart forsakes him who made him' (Ecclus. 10.7, 12).

It is the very opposite of that humble spirit which alone can learn true wisdom. We read that 'wisdom is far from *huperēphania*' (Ecclus. 15.8). *Huperēphania* was the characteristic of the proud men who so lifted themselves up that that God sent the flood upon the earth (Wisdom 14.6).

Of two men especially did the Jews use this word, for both these men had been guilty of the most terrible sacrilege, the sacrilege of entering the Holy of Holies, where none but the High Priest might go. They used the word of Antiochus Epiphanes who in insolence and *arrogance* tried to obliterate Jewish religion, and who entered the Holy Place and defiled the Temple (II Mac. 9.7). 'In his *huperēphania* he entered into the sanctuary' (I Mac. 1.21, 24).

And they used the words of Pompey, who, when he conquered Jerusalem, was guilty of the same sacrilege. 'When the sinful man *waxed proud* (*huperēphaneuesthai*, the corresponding verb), he cast down fenced walls with a battering-ram, and thou didst not prevent him. The heathen went up against thine altar; they trampled it down with their sandals in their *pride*' (Psalms of Solomon 2.1, 2). 'The adversary *wrought insolence* and his heart was alien from God' (Psalms of Solomon 17.15). 'Let God destroy all those who work iniquity with *insolence*' (Psalms of Solomon 4.28).

Huperēphania is the spirit which despises men and lifts itself arrogantly against God. No wonder Theophylact called *huperēphania* the *acropolis kakōn*, the peak of evils.

This pride can come from pride in birth, from pride in wealth, from pride in knowledge, from aristocratic pride, from intellectual pride, from spiritual pride. It is described by Trench as 'human nature in battle array against God'.

There remains one thing to note. We have already studied the word *alazōn* which describes the *boaster*, the man who shouts his claims and pretensions so that all can hear. But *huperēphania* is worse than that, for the seat of *huperēphania* is in the heart.

The blustering, boasting *alazōn* is plain for all to see; but the *huperēphanos* is the man who might well go about the world with downcast eyes and folded hands and with outward quietness, but with a silent contempt within his heart for his fellow-men; the *huperēphanos* is the man who might walk in outward humility, but in inward pride.

His basic sin is that he has forgotten that he is a creature and that God is the Creator; for the *huperēphanos* has erected an altar to himself within his own heart, and worships there.

KALOS

THE WORD OF WINSOMENESS

K A L O S is a characteristic NT word to describe a characteristic quality of the Christian life. In the NT *kalos* occurs no fewer than 100 times. Usually in the AV it is simply translated *good*, although occasionally it is translated *honest* (e.g., Rom. 12.17; II Cor. 8.21).

Honest in this connection does not primarily mean *telling the truth;* it is used in the Latin sense of *honestus,* which means, *handsome, gracious, fair to look upon.*

In classical Greek *kalos* is one of the noblest of words; and all through its history it never loses a certain splendour.

Originally it referred to *beauty of form.* It could be applied to any person who was lovely or to any thing that was beautiful. Candaules believed his queen to be the *fairest (kallistē,* the superlative) of all women (Herodotus, 1.8).

In Homer Nireus is the *comeliest (kallistos)* man of all the Greeks who came to Troy *(Iliad* 2.673). Athene the goddess appeared to Odysseus in the form of a woman *beautiful* and tall *(Odyssey* 13.289). When *kalos* describes persons in Homer it very often appears in company with *megas,* which means *tall.* There is stateliness in the beauty which *kalos* describes.

Xenophon describes Cyrus as *most handsome (kallistos)* in person, most generous in heart (Xenophon, *Cyropaedia* 1.2.1). In the *Memorabilia* Xenophon tells how Critobulus tells Socrates that he desires the skill to win a good soul and a *fair (kalos)* face (Xenophon, *Memorabilia* 2.6.30).

Kalos is used of any part of the body which is *fair* and *shapely.* Homer describes Menelaus with his *shapely (kalos)* legs and ankles stained with blood in the battle *(Iliad* 4.147); he speaks of the *fair (kalos)* flesh of Aphrodite the goddess of love *(Iliad* 5.354).

Kalos is used not only of persons; it can describe any thing which is *handsome* and *fair.* Homer uses it of a great and *goodly* court in a splendid house *(Odyssey* 14.7). He uses it of a beautifully wrought shield *(Iliad* 11.33); of the *fair* cloak and tunic which Circe brought to Odysseus *(Odyssey* 10.365); or a robe made for the goddess Athene, *fairest* in its broiderings *(Iliad* 6.224); of a *fair* tract of orchard land *(Iliad* 12.314).

Wherever this word is found there is the idea of loveliness, of attractiveness, of graciousness, of that which delights the heart and gives pleasure to the eyes.

Further, *kalos* is the adjective which implies love and admiration. Her citizens who loved her called Athens *the Beautiful* (*kalos*). Aristophanes tells how Sitalces, as a lover would, writes on the walls of the city : ' Athens is *beautiful* ' (*Acharnians* 144).

Pindar speaks of ' inglorious old age reft of all share of *blessings* ' (*Olymp.* 1.84). Xenophon tells how Croesus promised the Lydians, when he became king, that whatever *fair possessions* man or woman had would come to them (Xenophon, *Cyropaedia* 7.2.13).

Herodotus uses *kalos* in an interesting way. Speaking of the essential modesty which should characterize life, he says : ' Men have long ago made *wise* (*kalos*) rules for our learning ' (Herodotus, 1.8). He says that, compared with the Persians, the barbarous Massagetae have no experience of the *gracious* (*kalos*) things of life (Herodotus, 1.207). *Kalos* describes the things which make life gracious and lovely and good to live.

Still further, although *kalos* has this essential idea of beauty, it also has the idea of *usefulness*. The beauty which *kalos* describes is not merely decorative; it is also useful to men. So Homer, describing Phæacia, says : ' A *fair* (*kalos*) harbour lies on each side of the city ' (*Odyssey* 6.263). He uses it of a *favourable* wind. ' They embarked and set sail from broad Crete with the North wind blowing fresh and *fair* (*kalos*) ' (*Odyssey* 14.299).

Thucydides uses *kalos* to describe a well situated camp (Thucydides, 5.60). Xenophon uses *kalos* to describe coins which are made of genuine silver and which are not counterfeit, debased, worn or clipped (*Memorabilia* 3.1.9). The Greeks often spoke of a *kalos chronos*, a *good time*, a *fitting* time to do something.

Kalos in Greek also means *beautiful* and *honourable* in the *moral* sense. Homer, speaking of rapacious men, says : ' It is not *honourable* (*kalos*) or just to rob the guests of Telemachus ' (*Odyssey* 20.294).

When Antigone desires to bury the body of her brother

Polyneices, although the giving of the last rites of love has been forbidden, and when she is warned that she will suffer for what she desires to do, her answer is: ' 'Tis *sweet* (*kalos*) to me to die in such employ' (Sophocles, *Antigone* 72).

Pindar speaks of 'the light of *noble* (*kalos*) deeds unquenchable for ever' (*Isthm.* 4.42). Xenophon speaks of Socrates as a pattern of *nobleness* (*kalos*) (Xenophon, *Symposium* 8.17). Virtue, he says, brings *honour* (*kalos*) to you, and good to the state (Xenophon, *Memorabilia* 3.5.28).

Plato uses it to describe the good conduct in a boy which is a credit to the city of Athens where he is brought up (Plato, *Symposium* 183d). Socrates, Xenophon says, discussed what is godly, what is ungodly; what is *beautiful* (*kalos*), and what is ugly (Xenophon, *Memorabilia* 1.1.16).

Chrysippus the Stoic held that all that is good is beautiful (Diogenes Laertius, 7.101). *Kalos* describes the beauty which lies in the deed which is honourable and fine.

We may best of all see the meaning of *kalos*, if we contrast it with *agathos* which is the common Greek word for *good*. *Agathos* is that which is practically and morally good; *kalos* is that which is not only practically and morally good, but that which is also aesthetically good, which is lovely and pleasing to the eye.

Hort, commenting on James 2.7, says: '*Kalos* is what is good as seen, as making a direct impression on those who come in contact with it—not only good in result, which would be *agathos*.' In the creation story when God looked at the world which he had made, he saw that it was *good* (Gen. 1.8), and *kalos* is the word which is used.

When a thing or a person is *agathos*, it or he is good in the moral and practical sense of the term, and in the result of its or his activity; but *kalos* adds to the idea of goodness the idea of beauty, of loveliness, of graciousness, of winsomeness. *Agathos* appeals to the moral sense; but *kalos* appeals also to the eye.

Aristotle defines nobility (*to kalon*) as that which is agreeable or desirable in itself (*Rhetoric* 1364b 27). He describes it as being at one and the same time agreeable in itself and worthy of praise, as being good and pleasant (*ibid.* 1366a 33).

Latin translates this word *kalos* by the word *honestus*; and Cicero defines that which is *honestus* as being 'such that, even if its utility is taken away, and even if any rewards and fruits which come from it are removed, it can still be praised for its own sake' (*De Fin.* 2.45).

Tacitus describes the quality in *honestus* as 'that quality which makes a man worthy of praise, even if you strip him of everything else' (*Histories* 4.5). In anything that is *kalos* or *honestus* there is an innate and indestructible loveliness and attraction.

We may very briefly look at the use of this word in the papyri. It is used to describe animals which are in good condition and of gentle nature; it is used to describe drugs which are in good condition and efficient in contrast with drugs which have lost their efficacy. It is used to describe grapes· which are fully ripe, sweet to the taste and beautiful to look upon. It is used to describe wine which has been left to settle and to mature until it is mellow and at its best.

It is used to describe a *favourable* sale, a *well-cut* tunic. In describing people it is joined with *pistos*, which means *dependable* and *reliable*. It is used of *honourable* men whose word and pledge and oath can be unquestionably accepted. In discussing *kalos* in the papyri Milligan speaks of the *self-evidencing* power which is in *kalos*. That which is *kalos* bears its goodness on its face.

Clearly *kalos* is a noble word. It describes that which is beautiful, that which commands love and admiration, that which is useful, that which is honourable. *Kalos* is the word of the goodness which is a lovely thing, the goodness which not only satisfies the conscience, but which also delights the heart, and gives pleasure to the eyes.

Having studied the word *kalos* in classical Greek and in the papyri, we now turn to its usage in the NT.

(i) *Kalos* is used in the NT as it is in secular Greek, to describe things which are useful for all the purposes of life and which are pleasant to see. It describes the stones of which the Temple is built (Luke 21.5). It describes the fruit which the fruitful and the good tree produces (Matt. 3.10; cp. Luke 3.9; Matt. 7.17-19; 12.33; Luke 6.43). It describes the *good* ground which is clean and rich and fertile (Matt. 13.8, 23; cp. Mark 4.8, 20 and Luke 8.15). It describes the *good* seed which is sown into the ground (Matt. 13.24, 27, 37, 38). It described the *good* and *useful* fish which are caught in the assortment which the dragnet brings in (Matt. 13.48). Salt is said to be *kalos* (Mark 9.50). It describes *good* wine (John 2.10). It describes the *good* measure which is generously given (Luke 6.38). The Law is *kalos* (Rom. 7.16; I Tim. 1.8). The name of Christ is *kalos* (James 2.7). The word of God is *kalos* (Heb. 5.14). *Kalos* is the word which characteristically describes the good and useful and pleasant things of life.

(ii) One of the most interesting and significant uses of *kalos* is that it is repeatedly and consistently used to describe the *good deeds* which should characterize the life of the Christian. Our light is so to shine before men that they may see our *good deeds* (Matt. 5.16). Jesus has shown His enemies many *good works* (John 10.32, 33).

Paul can will, but cannot do *to kalon*, that which is *good* (Rom. 7.16). The Corinthians must do that which is *kalos* (II Cor. 13.7). The Galatians must not grow weary in doing what is *kalos* (Gal. 6.9). The Thessalonians must test all things, and hold fast to that which is *kalos* (I Thess. 5.21).

The Christian must be an example of, and zealous for, *good works* (Titus 2.7, 14). He must be anxious to produce *good works*, by which his life must be marked (Titus 3.8, 14). Christians must incite each other to love and *good works* (Heb. 10.24); and they must have a *good* conscience (Heb. 13.18).

Here is a use of the word *kalos* which sheds a flood of light on the Christian life. Clearly it is not enough that the Christian life should be good; it must also be attractive. A grim and unlovely goodness is certainly goodness, but it is not *Christian* goodness; for Christian goodness must have a certain loveliness on it. On Christian good works there must be the bloom of charm. Real Christianity must always attract and never repel. There is such a thing as a hard, austere, unlovely and unlovable goodness, but such a goodness falls far short of the Christian standard. In all his efforts to be good, in all his strivings towards moral holiness, the Christian must never forget the *beauty of holiness*.

(iii) From this basic idea of the word *kalos* there follows an appeal which runs through the whole NT. The NT, if we may use an ugly phrase, stresses again and again the propaganda value of the truly Christian life. It stresses the fact that the best advocate of Christianity to the outsider is the sheer attractive loveliness of the life of the true Christian.

It is Paul's advice to the Romans that they should provide things *honest* (*kalos*) in the sense of the Latin *honestus*, i.e., handsome, fair to look upon, in the sight of all men (Rom. 12.17). He urges the Corinthians to provide things that are *honest* (*kalos*), not only in the sight of God, but also in the sight of men (II Cor. 8.21).

The Pastoral Epistles insist that the office-bearers of the Church must have a *good* report from those who are *outside* the Church (I Tim. 3.7). The widows must have a public reputation for *good* works (I Tim. 5.10). A Christian's only wealth and foundation must lie in *good* works (I Tim. 6.18).

James urges men to live a way of life which proves and demonstrates their faith (James 3.13). Peter urges his converts to make their way of life *kalos* among the Gentiles (I Peter 2.12).

The NT holds that the best missionary weapon which the

Church possesses is the truly Christian life. It holds that men are to be *attracted*, far more than argued, into the Christian life. There should be in the life of the Christian not only a goodness, but also a loveliness, which will make all men who see it desire the secret which is his.

It is one of the most suggestive and the most illuminating facts about the word *kalos* that, out of its 100 appearances in the NT, 24 are in the Pastoral Epistles.

These letters to Timothy and to Titus were written at a crucial time in the history of the Church. They were written when the Church was a little island of Christianity surrounded by a sea of paganism. They were written at a time when the Church's missionary task was at its most demanding and its most difficult. To meet that situation every person in the Church, and every action of every person in the Church had to be *kalos*. The world had to be presented with the loveliness, the winsomeness, the attractiveness of the Christian faith. We might almost say that men had to be charmed into Christianity.

(i) Office in the Church must be *kalos* (I Tim. 3.1; 3.13). Too often office in the Church is characterized by criticism, obstructiveness, self-righteousness and self-importance; it it ought to be characterized by the loveliness of service, encouragement, support and love.

(ii) The Christian is to be a *good* soldier and he is to fight a *good* campaign, which indeed Paul was able to claim that he himself had done (I Tim. 1.18; 6.12; II Tim. 2.3; 4.7). There must be a quality of chivalrous gallantry about the Christian life. The Christian must not serve like a conscript, press-ganged into the service of Christ; he must be the adventurer of Christ. He must make it clear to all by his vital happiness that he finds the service of Christ a thrilling thing, even when it is hard and difficult. The Christian must be the laughing cavalier of Christ.

(iii) The Christian must be the *good* servant of Jesus Christ (I Tim. 4.6). The service of the Christian both to Christ and to his fellow men must be service with a smile, the service of the extra mile, the service given always without a grudge, the service in which the servant obviously finds pleasure and delight. It is not enough to serve Christ efficiently; to the efficiency there must be added the charm and the loveliness which *kalos* always includes.

(iv) The Christian teaching must be *kalos* (I Tim. 4.6). In all Christian teaching, even at its sternest, there must be charm and attractiveness. Robert Louis Stevenson notes in his diary; as if it was a most unusual event: 'Went to church to-day and was not depressed.' Clovis G. Chappell says: 'No man has a right so to preach as to send his hearers away on flat tyres. . . . Every discouraging sermon is a wicked sermon. . . . A discouraged man is not an asset but a liability.' The Christian teaching must be *kalos*; it must woo men, not bludgeon or threaten men, to Christ.

(v) The Christian witness and profession must be *kalos*, as indeed was the witness of Jesus Christ himself (I Tim. 6.12, 13). A man can witness for Christ in such a way that he attracts his fellow men; and he can witness for Christ in such a way that he repels his fellow men. True Christian witness is not a grim, austere thing, full of protests and prohibitions, a thing which emasculates the vitality and obliterates the colour of life. True Christian witness attracts by its radiance, its vitality, its vividness. One of her pupils said of Alice Freeman Palmer, the great teacher: 'She made me feel as if I were bathed in sunshine.' That is the effect that true Christian witness ought to have.

(vi) To the material of the Pastoral Epistles, First Peter has one thing to add: the steward of the grace of God must be *kalos* (I Peter 4.10). It is the duty of the Christian to bring to his fellow men the grace of God; and especially that is the duty of the minister of Christ and of his Church. He must do so with charm and attractiveness. His first instinct must be, not to shut the door, but to open the door, not to condemn, but always to sympathize. There are preachers who preach with such threats and such denunciation that when we listen to them we almost feel that they hate us; no preacher will ever win men for Christ unless he first makes it clear that he loves them. There must be a certain graciousness in him who would be the steward of the grace of God, if he is to merit the title of *kalos*, which ought to belong to him.

Every Christian should be *kalos*; and every activity of the Christian life should be *kalos*. The Christian should be clad with a mantle of graciousness, and his every action should radiate winsomeness; only so will he serve Christ and win his fellow men.

We have studied the meaning and usage of the word *kalos* in classical Greek and in the NT in some detail; but we have deliberately left to the end the two usages of it in the NT which illustrates its meaning best of all.

One of the loveliest stories in the NT is the story of the anointing of Jesus' head by the woman in the house of Simon the leper at Bethany. The woman loved Jesus, and this was the only way in which she could show her love. The dull, insensitive, unimaginative spectators criticized her for the reckless extravagance of what she had done. Jesus' answer was: 'She hath wrought a *good, kalos,* work upon me' (Matt. 26.10; cp. Mark 14.6).

That incident is the perfect illustration of all that *kalos* means. It was a demonstration of love; it was the act of a love which knew that only the best it had to give was good enough; it was the act of a love which refused to count the cost. It was the act of a love which set beauty far above mere utility; of a love which knew that giving can never be dictated by the cautious prudentialities of common sense. A deed which is *kalos* is a deed in which there is enshrined the beauty of love's extravagance.

The second usage in the NT which demonstrates the meaning of *kalos* is that it is the word which is used of Jesus in that title which is for many the most precious title of Jesus—the *Good* Shepherd (John 10.11, 14).

The shepherd does not look after his sheep with only a cold efficiency. He looks after them with a sacrificial love.

When the sheep are in trouble, he does not nicely calculate the risk of helping them; he gives his life for the sheep. He does not give so many hours' service to the sheep per day, and carefully calculate that he must work so many hours a week. All through the day he watches over them, and all through the night he lies across the opening in the sheep-fold so that he is literally the door. Here we have the same idea again. The *good* shepherd is the shepherd whose service is a lovely and an heroic things because it is a service, not rendered for pay, but rendered for love.

The basic idea in the word *kalos* is the idea of winsome beauty; and we are bound to see that nothing can be *kalos* unless it be the product of love. Deeds which are *kalos* are the outcome of a heart in which love reigns supreme. The outward beauty of the deed springs from the inward magnitude of the love within the heart.

There is no English word which fully translates *kalos*; there is no word which gathers up within itself the beauty, the winsomeness, the attractiveness, the generosity, the usefulness, which are all included in this word. Perhaps the word which comes nearest to it is the Scots word *bonnie*.

J. P. Struthers, that great Scottish preacher, used to say that it would do the Church more good than anything else in the world if Christians would only sometimes do a *bonnie* thing. He lived up to his own teaching. He lived in a manse in Greenock which was at the end of the road which led up to the hillside above the firth. The lads and lasses used to take that road at evening time. Struthers had a garden; and he used to pluck the flowers in it and make them up into little posies which he used to lay along his garden wall. And the lads knew that he meant them to take the posies and give them to the girls with whom they were walking along the road. That was an action which was the perfect illustration of this word *kalos*; and that is the kind of action which does the Church more good than most of the great works of theology that ever were written.

Scholarship can baffle; learning can bewilder; efficiency can chill; aggressiveness can antagonize. That which tugs at men's hearts and pulls them to Christ is the winsome attractiveness in Jesus Christ himself, the attractiveness which ought to reside in those who claim to be his.

If we would serve Christ in his Church, there must be on our lives that winsome beauty which will entitle us, too, to the title of *kalos*, loveliest of all the words which describe the Christian life.

KATAGGELLEIN

THE WORD OF AUTHORITY

THE word *kataggellein* means to *announce* or *to proclaim*; but the characteristic flavour of the word is that the announcement or the proclamation is made *with authority*. In classical Greek it is used of *proclaiming war* or *announcing a festival*.

In the papyri a widow makes an official *pronouncement* regarding the appointment of a representative to look after her interests in consequence of her husband's death. It is used of the *announcement* of an emperor's accession to the throne. Always the word carries with it weight and authority.

In the NT the word is used 15 times. It is used of the prophets *foretelling* the coming of Christ and the events of the early days (Acts 3.24). It is used of the work of Jesus in that he *showed* light to the people and to the Gentiles (Acts 26.23). It is Paul's word of praise that the faith of of the Roman church is *spoken* of throughout the world (Rom. 1.8). The words and actions of the Sacrament are said to *show forth* the death of Christ (I Cor. 11.26).

But the main interest of the word lies in the fact that it is one of the great NT words for *preaching*. In Acts 15.36 we are told that Paul and Barnabas plan to revisit the churches to which they have *preached* (*kataggellein*).

Now the interest of the word lies in the examination of *the things which were preached*, for these are the things which are proclaimed *with authority*. What then were the things which the early preachers preached with authority, the things they preached as certainties, the things they preached as part of the unalterable and authoritative message of the Christian faith?

(i) They proclaimed *the word of God*. It is said that Paul and Barnabas *preached* (*kataggellein*) the word of God in the synagogues of Cyprus (Acts 13.5). It was the word of God that Paul *preached* at Berea (Acts 17.13). Preaching is not the proclamation of a preacher's private opinions; still less is it the public airing of his doubts; it is the proclamation of the word of God. 'Tell me of your certainties,' said Goethe, 'I have doubts enough of my own.'

(ii) They proclaimed *Christ*. Paul does not care how the preaching is done so long as Christ is *preached* (Phil. 1.16, 18). It is Christ whom he himself *preached* (Col. 1.28). In the early days the preachers did not deal with things on the circumference of the faith; they proclaimed the facts of the life, and the death, and the resurrection of Jesus Christ. Their primary aim was to confront men with Christ.

(iii) They proclaimed through Jesus *the resurrection from the dead* (Acts 4.2). The message of the preacher was the defeat of death. They preached a risen Christ, and they preached a life that was indestructible.

(iv) They proclaimed *the Messiahship of Jesus*. It was Paul's message that 'this Jesus whom I *preach* to you is Christ' (Acts 17.3). It was the message of the early preachers that in this man Jesus God's promises were fulfilled, that eternity had invaded time, that heaven's rule had begun.

(v) They proclaimed that *the way was open to the God whom men had ever sought but never found*. It was Paul's proclamation that he brought to the Athenians news of the

God who to them had always been the unknown God
(Acts 17.23). The time of guessing and groping had gone,
and the time of knowing had come. The time of searching
was ended, and the time of finding had come. George
Borrow tells us that once when he was on one of his tours
he was surrounded by some gipsies, who cried out: 'Give
us God! Give us God!' Not knowing what to do, he put
his hand in his pocket and scattered some money amongst
them. But they disregarded the money. 'Not your money,'
they said. 'Give us God!' It was God whom the early
preachers claimed to give to men.

(vi) They proclaimed *a gospel*. It was the gospel which
the preacher preached; it was good news (I Cor. 9.14). Any
preaching which ultimately depresses a man is wrong, for
preaching may begin by cutting a man to the heart with
the sight and the realization of his sins; but it must end
by leading him to the love, the forgiveness and the grace
of God.

The very word which is so often used for preaching
shows that in the early preaching there was nothing
apologetic, nothing diffident, nothing clouded with doubts
and misted with uncertainties. It was preaching with
authority; and the things it preached with authority are
still the basis of the message of the preacher to-day.

KATALLASSEIN

THE WORD OF RECONCILIATION

THERE is in the writings of Paul a group of words which
are of extreme importance, because he uses them to
express the central experience of the Christian faith.

All these words are compound forms made from the
simple verb *allassein* which means *to change*. In classical
Greek *allassein* itself can be used to express *changing* shape,

or colour, or appearance. It can also be used in the sense of to *exchange* or to *barter*; and it can frequently be used of *taking one thing in exchange for another*. It is, for instance, used of one who in misfortune exchanges one sorrow for another.

This simple verb *allassein* is not uncommon in the NT. Stephen is charged with teaching that Jesus will *change* the accepted customs of the Jews (Acts 6.14). The heathen have *changed* the glory of God for lifeless, corrupted and polluted images (Rom. 1.23). Paul tells the people of Corinth that we shall all be *changed* (I Cor. 15.51). When Paul realizes the danger of perversion of the faith among the Galatians, he wishes to *change* his voice, and to adopt the accent of sternness and rebuke (Gal. 4.20). The word is used of *changing* a garment in Heb. 1.12. *Allassein* then can be used of almost any kind of *change*.

This word *allassein* acquires certain compound forms. In ordinary classical Greek the commonest of the compound forms is the form *katallassein*, and *katallassein* is one of the great Pauline words also. But we must go on with the examination of this group of words in ordinary secular Greek before we come to their use in the NT.

Katallassein in ordinary secular Greek acquires the almost technical sense of *changing money*, or *changing into money*. Plutarch tells how four Syrian brothers stole the king's gold vessels in Corinth and how bit by bit they *changed* them into money (Plutarch, *Aratus* 18). The corresponding noun *katallagē* has the same sense of *exchange*, especially the exchange of money.

Katallassein then begins to acquire a wider sense of exchanging any one thing for another. Aristotle, for instance, speaks of professional and mercenary soldiers who are willing to *barter* their lives for trifling gain (Aristotle, *Nicomachean Ethics* 1117b 20).

But then *katallassein* takes a still further step and it begins to mean, more than anything else, *the change of enmity into friendship*. Clytæmnestra reminds Agamemnon

how he had been responsible for the death of her former
husband and her children and then says: 'Reconciled to
thee and to thy house, a blameless wife was I' (Euripides,
Iphigeneia at Aulis 1157). Sophocles speaks of a man
making his peace with heaven (Sophocles, *Ajax* 744).
Thucydides tells how in the Sicilian wars Hermocrates pled
with the warring sections to set aside conflicting claims,
and become *reconciled* with each other (Thucydides, 4.59).
Xenophon tells of a man who had made war on Cyrus and
who had then *become his friend again* (Xenophon, *Anabasis* 1.6.1). In all these cases the verb is *katallassein*.

So then in classical Greek *katallassein* becomes characteristically the word of the bringing together again of
people who have been estranged. In a papyrus a man who
is apparently a father who has had a difference with a
member of his family, asks the question from an oracle:
'Am I to be *reconciled* to my offspring?'

Even before the NT used it *katallassein* is the word of
reconciliation.

We now turn to *katallassein* and to its kindred words in
the NT. With only two exceptions these words are used
always of the restoration of the relationship between man
and God.

The first exception is I Cor. 7.11 where Paul lays it
down that a woman who has left her husband must not
marry another, but must be *reconciled* to him. The other
case is the single usage in the NT of the kindred word
sunallassein. It is used in Acts 7.26 of Moses when he
tried *to set at one* the two Israelites who were quarrelling
in Egypt. Even when this word is used in connection with
human relationships, it always refers to the restoration of
a broken friendship and an interrupted fellowship.

It is only Paul who uses this group of words in the NT;
and he always uses these words of the restoration of the
relationship between man and God.

In Rom. 5.11 he speaks of Jesus Christ through whom
we have now received the *atonement* (*katallagē*). In Rom.

11.15 he explains the casting away of the Jews by saying that that casting away was necessary for the *reconciling* of the world (*katallagē*). In II Cor. 5.18, 19 he speaks of the ministry and the word of *reconciliation* (*katallagē*).

In Rom. 5.10 he says that while we were enemies we were *reconciled* to God by the death of his Son (*katallassein*). In II Cor. 5.18-20 there is a whole series of uses of this word. God has *reconciled* us to himself by Jesus. God was in Christ *reconciling* the world unto himself. We pray you to be *reconciled* to God.

Twice Paul uses a kind of intensified form of this word, *apokatallassein*. In Eph. 2.16 he tells how Jesus Christ has *reconciled* Jews and Gentiles to each other, and both to God; and in Col. 1.21 he tells how Jesus Christ has *reconciled* all things and all men to God.

(i) First and foremost, Paul sees the work of Jesus Christ as above and beyond all else a work of reconciliation. Through that which he did, the lost relationship between man and God is restored. Man was made for friendship and fellowship with God. By his disobedience and rebellion he ended up at enmity with God. That which Jesus did took that enmity away, and restored the relationship of friendship which should always have existed, but which was broken by man's sin.

(ii) It is to be carefully noted that Paul never speaks of God being reconciled to men, but always of men being reconciled to God. The most significant of all the passages, II Cor. 5.18-20, three times speaks of God reconciling man to himself. It was man, not God, who needed to be reconciled. Nothing had lessened the love of God; nothing had turned that love to hate; nothing had ever banished that yearning from the heart of God. Man might sin, but God still loved. It was not God who needed to be pacified, but man who needed to be moved to surrender and to penitence and to love.

(iii) Here then we are face to face with an inescapable truth. The effect of the Cross—at least in this sphere of the thought of Paul—was on man, and not on God. The effect of the Cross changed, not the heart of God, but the heart of man. It was man who needed to be reconciled, not God. It is entirely against all Pauline thought to think of Jesus Christ pacifying an angry God, or to think that in some way God's wrath was turned to love, and God's judgment was turned to mercy, because of something which Jesus did.

When we look at it in Paul's way, it was man's sin which was turned to penitence, man's rebellion which was turned to surrender, man's enmity which was turned to love, by the sacrificial love of Jesus Christ upon the Cross. It cost that Cross to make that change in the hearts of men.

(iv) One thing remains to be said. If all this is so—and it is so—the ministry of the Church is a ministry of reconciliation, as indeed Paul said it was (II Cor. 5.19, 20). The function of the preacher is to convey to men, not the announcement of the threat of God's wrath, but the proclamation of the offer of God's love. The message of the preacher must ever be: Look at that Cross and see how much God loves you. Can you hold back in face of a love like that?

The very essence of Christianity is the restoration of a lost relationship. The summons of Christianity is to return to a God whose love men spurned, but whose love is ever waiting for men to come home. The task of the preacher is to break men's hearts at the sight of the broken heart of God.

LOGOS

THE WORD OF THE
CHRISTIAN MESSAGE

THE word *logos* means *word*. The Fourth Gospel uses *logos* in a technical sense when it calls Jesus *The Word*; but before we come to that special usage we wish to study its ordinary usage in the NT. Naturally it is one of the commonest of all Greek words, but, common as it is, the more we study it, the more we shall see a wealth of meaning.

Ho logos, the word, becomes almost a synonym for the Christian *message*. Mark tells us that Jesus preached the *word* to the crowds (Mark 2.2). In the parable the seed that the sower sowed was *the word* (Mark 4.14). It was the work of Paul and his friends to preach *the word* (Acts 14.25). Most often this word is said to be *the word of God* (Luke 5.1; 11.28; John 10.35; Acts 4.31; 6.7; 13.44; I Cor. 14.36; Heb. 13.7). Sometimes it is *the word of the Lord* (I Thess. 4.15; II Thess. 3.1). And once it is *the word of Christ* (Col. 3.16). Now genitives in Greek can be either *subjective* or *objective*. If these genitives are *subjective* the phrases mean the word which God gave, the word which the Lord gave, and the word which Christ gave. If they are *objective*, they mean the word which tells about God, or about the Lord, or about Christ. In all probability both the subjective and the objective meanings are involved in these phrases. This means to say that the Christian message, the *logos, the word*, is something which came from God; it is not the discovery of man, but the gift of God; and it is something which tells about God, something which man could not have discovered for himself.

The very fact that the word *logos* is used for the Christian message is very significant. It means *a spoken message*, and therefore it means that the Christian message is not something which is learned from books, but something which is transmitted from person to person. Papias, the second-century Christian writer, says that he learned more from the living and abiding voice than from any book. The Christian message comes far more often through the living personality than through the printed or the written page.

This *word*, this *logos*, has certain functions.

(i) The word *judges* (John 12.48). An old catechism asks what will happen if the truths recounted in it are disregarded. Its answer is that condemnation will follow, and a condemnation all the greater because the reader has read this book. To have heard the truth is not only to have received a privilege; it is also to have had a responsibility laid upon us.

(ii) The word *purifies* (John 15.3; I Tim. 4.5). It purifies by exposing evil and by pointing to good. It rebukes that which is wrong and exhorts to that which is right. It purifies in the negative sense by seeking to eradicate old faults; and it purifies in the positive sense by exhorting to new virtues.

(iii) Through the word *belief* comes (Acts 4.4). No man can believe in the Christian message until he has heard the Christian message. The word is that which gives a man the opportunity to believe; and, having heard the word himself, there is laid upon him the duty of giving others the same chance to hear it, that they also may believe.

(iv) The word is *the agent of rebirth* (I Peter 1.23). One thing is true, as G. K. Chesterton said, 'Whatever man is, he is not what he was meant to be.' He has to be changed so radically that the change can only be called a new birth, and the word is the first agent in that tremendous re-creating change.

The study of the word *logos* becomes of primary importance when we study what the NT says we must do with this *logos*.

(i) The *logos* must be *heard* (Matt. 13.20; Acts 13.7; 13.44). The duty of listening is laid upon the Christian. Among the many voices of the world he must tune his ears to hear the message which is the message of God. He will never give himself the opportunity to know unless he gives himself the opportunity to hear.

(ii) The *logos* must be *received* (Luke 8.13; James 1.21; Acts 8.14; 11.1; 17.11). There is a hearing which is a purely external thing. Either the tide of words flows over the

hearer and his hearing leaves no effect upon him, or he listens and dismisses the whole matter as having nothing to do with him. The Christian message must not only be listened to, but must be taken into the heart and mind and inwardly digested.

(iii) The *logos* must be *held on to* (Luke 8.13). The Greeks described time by an adjective which means 'time which wipes all things out'. Any word can be heard, and for a time accepted, and then obliterated by the passage of time. The Christian message must be deliberately retained. It must be held in the forefront of the mind, thought about, meditated on, so that it is retained and not lost.

(iv) The *logos* is something *to abide in* (John 8.31). There is always a circle of thoughts and ideas in which a man lives and moves and has his being; in which he rests his life and by which he directs his activities. The Christian message must be the thing in which and by which a man lives.

(v) The *logos* must be *kept* (John 8.51, 14.23; I John 2.5; Rev. 3.8). It is a message which is not knowledge for the mind alone; it is direction for life. It issues not in speculation but in action. Its demand is obedience. It is not only a knowledge to think about; it is an ethic and a law to be obeyed.

(vi) The *logos* must be *witnessed to* (Acts 8.25; Rev. 1.2). It is something to which a man's whole life must bear witness. He can only prove that he has accepted it by living it. It is something which in any society he must be prepared to show that he accepts. It is something of which his whole life and action must say, 'I know and bear witness that this is true.'

(vii) The *logos* is something which must be *served* (Acts 6.4). It is something which brings its duties. It is not only something which a man accepts for himself, but something which he is bound to wish to bring to others. It is not only something which brings wealth to his own soul; it is also something for which he must be prepared to spend his whole life.

(viii) The *logos* is something which must be *announced*. Two words are specially used. II Tim. 4.2 uses the word *kērussein*, which is the word that is used for a herald making a proclamation. Acts 15.36 and 17.13 use the word *kataggellein* which is the word that is used for making an official and an authoritative pronouncement. The proclamation must be made with authority and with certainty. The proclamation is so made because, when we announce the Christian message to others, we are not saying, 'I am saying this,' we are saying, 'Thus saith the Lord.'

(ix) The *logos* must be spoken *with boldness* (Acts 4.29; Phil. 1.14). Some time ago a book was published with the suggestive title, *No More Apologies*. It may well be that we have been too anxious to meet the world halfway, that we have tried too much to attune the Christian message to the world's ears, that we have watered it down, and emasculated it in order to make it less demanding and therefore more attractive. There should be a certain un-compromising quality in our proclamation of the *logos*.

(x) The *logos* must be *taught* (Acts 18.11). The Christian message begins with proclamation, but it must go on to explanation. One of the gravest weaknesses of the Church is that so many people do not know what Christianity really means and believes and stands for; and one of the gravest faults in preaching is that it so often exhorts a man to be a Christian without teaching him what Christianity is. Teaching is an essential part of the Christian message.

(xi) The *logos* must be *acted upon* (James 1.22). The Christian message is not something exclusively for the calm of the study, for the dissection of the lecture room, for the mental acrobatics of the discussion group. It is something which has to be lived out in day-to-day living.

(xii) The *logos* may involve *persecution and suffering* (I Thess. 1.6; Rev. 1.9). It is not likely that in this country we shall have to die for our faith; but we shall have to live for it, and there may well be times when we have to choose between what is easy and what is right.

If our relationship to the *logos* involves obligations, it will inevitably be liable to failures.

(i) The *logos* may be *disbelieved* (I Peter 2.8). It may be disbelieved either because the hearer thinks it too good to be true, or because, in wishful thinking, he does not want it to be true, because it condemns his life and seeks to change him.

(ii) The *logos* can both be *snatched away* and *choked* (Matt. 13.22; cp. Mark 4.15). The temptations, the impulses and the passions of life can make a man forget the Christian message as soon as he has heard it. The activities, the cares and the pleasures of life can take up so much of a man's life and time that the Christian message is choked out of his life because there is no room left for it to breathe.

(iii) The *logos* can be *corrupted* and *adulterated* (II Cor. 2.17; 4.2). Whenever a man begins to listen to himself and stops listening to God, his version of the Christian message will be distorted and inadequate. Whenever he forgets to test his ideas and conceptions by the Word and the Spirit of God, he will produce a version of the Christian message which is his and not God's. If he goes on doing that he may well end by loving his own little system better than he loves God's truth.

(iv) The *logos* can be rendered *ineffective* (Mark 7.13). It is fatally easy to explain the Christian message away, to overlay it with human interpretations, to complicate its simplicities with conditions and reservations and explanations. Whenever we regard the Christian message as something with which to make terms rather than something to which to surrender we are in danger of making it ineffective. Without ' yieldedness ' to the message the message cannot have its full effect.

When we begin to examine the NT content of the Christian message, we begin to appreciate, as never before, the riches of this faith which is offered to us. The word *logos* is used in the NT with at least seven different genitives which express that in which the message consists. Let us look at them.

(i) The Christian message is *a word of good news* (Acts 15.7). It brings to us tidings about God which set the heart singing for joy. The discovery of love is always the greatest day in a man's life; and the Christian message leads a man to discover nothing less than the love of God.

(ii) The Christian message is *a word of truth* (John 17.7; Eph. 1.13; James 1.8). The whole of life is the search for truth. 'What is truth?' said jesting Pilate, and would not stay for an answer. That may be so, but life is intolerable if there are no fixed stars in it. The Christian message is that which makes a man sure.

(iii) The Christian message is *a word of life* (Phil. 2.16). The Christian message is that which enables a man to stop existing and to begin living. It gives him life with a capital L.

(iv) The Christian message is *a word of righteousness* (Heb. 5.13). It tells a man where goodness lies; it shows him what goodness is; it gives him new standards for life; and it enables him to reach them and gives him the power which is not his own power to achieve them.

(v) The Christian message is *a word of reconciliation* (II Cor. 5.19). The very essence of it is that God is not our enemy but our friend. It is not that God needed to be reconciled to us; the NT never puts it that way; it is we who needed to be reconciled to God. The great gift of the Christian message is that it removes the estrangement between man and God and makes possible the greatest friendship of all.

(vi) The Christian message is *a word of salvation* (Acts 13.26). It is a word of rescue. It rescues a man from the evil bonds which bind him. It strengthens him to defeat the temptations of evil and to do the right. It rids him of the punishment which is his by right, if God were to treat him only with justice and not with love. It lifts a man out of the deadly situation in which he finds himself in this life, and in which he ought in justice to find himself in the life to come.

(vii) The Christian message is *a word of the Cross* (I Cor. 1.18). It is the story of one who died for men. It is the story of a love which did not stop until it reached the very limits of sacrifice, and which thereby proved that there is nothing that God will not dare and suffer and sacrifice for the sake of man. The heart of the Christian *logos* is the Cross.

In the NT there is one technical use of the word *logos*. It occurs in the Prologue to the Fourth Gospel, and it culminates in that great saying, 'The *Word* (*logos*) was made flesh and dwelt among us' (John 1.14). This is one of the greatest sayings in the NT and we shall have to dig deep if we wish to grasp something of its meaning.

(i) We must begin by remembering that in Greek *logos* has two meanings. (a) It means *word*, and (b) it means *reason*, and these two meanings are always intertwined.

(ii) We must begin with the *Jewish* background of this idea. In Jewish thought a word was more than a sound expressing a meaning; *a word actually did things.* The word of God is not simply a sound; *it is an effective cause.* In the creation story God's *word creates.* God said, Let there be light, *and there was light.* (Gen. 1.3). By the *word* of the Lord the heavens were made . . . for he spake and it was done (Ps. 33.6, 9). He sent his *word* and healed them (Ps. 107.20). God's *word* will accomplish that which God pleases (Is. 55.11). Always we must remember that in Jewish thought God's *word* not only *said* things; it *did* things.

(iii) There came a time when the Jews forgot their Hebrew; their language became Aramaic. It was necessary that the scriptures should be translated into Aramaic. These translations are called the Targums. Now in the simplicity of the OT human feelings, actions, reactions, thoughts are ascribed to God. The makers of the Targums felt that this was far too human; and in such cases they used a circumlocution for the name of God. They spoke not of God but of the *Word*, the *memra* of God. This is the kind of thing that happened. In Ex. 19.17 the Targums say that Moses brought the people out of the camp to meet with the *memra*, the *Word* of God, instead of, quite simply, with God. In Deut. 9.3 it is God's *Word*, the *memra*, which is a consuming fire. In Isa. 48.13 we read, Mine hand hath laid the foundations of the earth; and my right hand hath spanned the heavens. In the Targums this becomes, By my *Word*, my *memra*, I have founded the earth, and by my strength I have hung up the heavens. The result of all this was that the Jewish scriptures in their popular form became full of the phrase, The *Word*, the *memra*, of God; and the word was always *doing* things; not merely *saying* things.

(iv) Now let us remember that *Word* and *Reason* are locked together. In Jewish thought there is another great conception—the conception of *Wisdom* (*sophia*). This is specially so in the Old Testament in Proverbs. By *Wisdom* God founded the earth (Prov. 3.13-20). The great passage is in Prov. 8.1-9. There wisdom is from everlasting, before the earth came into being: she was with God in the day of creation. This idea was much developed in the books between the Testaments. In Ecclus. 1.1-10 there is the picture of *Wisdom* who was created before all things and who is intertwined with creation. In the Wisdom of Solomon, *Wisdom works* all things (8.5). God made all things by his *Word* and man by his *Wisdom* (9.1, 2). *Wisdom* was God's instrument in creation and is woven throughout all the world.

So in Jewish thought we have two great conceptions at the back of the idea of Jesus as the *Word*, the *logos* of God. First, God's *Word* is not only *speech*; it is *power*. Second, it is impossible to separate the ideas of *Word* and *Wisdom*; and it was God's *Wisdom* which created and permeated the world which God made.

By the end of the first century the Christian Church was faced with an acute problem in communication. The

Church had been cradled in Judaism, but now she had to present her message to a Greek world, to which the categories of Judaism were quite alien. As Goodspeed puts it: 'A Greek who felt like becoming a Christian was called upon to accept Jesus as the Christ, the Messiah. He would naturally ask what this meant, and would have to be given a short course in Jewish apocalyptic thought. Was there no way in which he might be introduced directly to the values of Christian civilization without being for ever routed, we might even say detoured, through Judaism? Must Christianity always speak in a Jewish vocabulary?' Round about A.D. 100 there was a man in Ephesus called John who saw this problem. His was perhaps the greatest mind in the Christian Church; and suddenly he saw the solution. *Both Jew and Greek possessed the conception of the logos of of God.* Could the two ideas not be brought together? Let us see the Greek background with which John had to work.

(i) Away back in 560 B.C. there was a Greek philosopher called Heracleitus, who also lived in Ephesus. He conceived of the world as what he called a *flux*. Everything is in a state of change; there is nothing static in the world. But if everything is changing all the time, why is the world not an absolute and complete chaos? His answer was that 'all things happen according to the *logos*.' In the world there is a reason and a mind at work; that mind is the mind of God, God's *logos*; and it is that *logos* which makes the world an ordered cosmos and not a disordered chaos.

(ii) This idea of a mind, a reason, a *logos* ruling the world fascinated the Greeks. Anaxagoras spoke of the mind (*nous*) which 'rules over all things'. Plato declared that it was God's *logos* which kept the planets in their courses, and brought back the seasons and the years in their appointed times. But it was the Stoics, who were at their strongest when the NT was being written, who passionately loved this conception. To them this *logos* of God, as Cleanthes said, 'roamed through all things'. The times, the seasons, the tides, the stars in their courses were ordered by the

logos; it was the *logos* which put sense into the world.
Further, the mind of man himself was a little portion of
this *logos*. 'Reason is nothing else than a part of the divine
spirit immersed in the human body,' said Seneca. It was the
logos which put sense into the universe and sense into
man; and this *logos* was nothing other than the mind of
God.

(iii) This conception was brought to its highest peak by
Philo, who was an Alexandrian Jew, and who had the aim
of joining together in one synthesis the highest thought of
Jew and Greek. To him the *logos* of God was ' inscribed and
engraved upon the constitution of all things.' The *logos* is
'the tiller by which the pilot of the universe steers all
things'. 'Every man is akin in understanding to the divine
logos.' 'The *logos* is the high priest which sets the soul
before God.' The *logos* is the bridge between man and God.

Now we can see what John was doing when he uttered
his tremendous statement, 'The *Word* was made flesh.'

(i) He was clothing Christianity in a dress that a Greek
could understand. Here is a challenge to us. He refused to
go on expressing Christianity in outworn and Judaistic
categories. He used categories that his age knew and understood. Again and again the Church has failed in that task
through mental laziness, through fear to cut adrift from
the past, through shrinking from possible heresy; but ' the
man who would discover a new continent must accept the
hazard of sailing upon an uncharted sea.' If we are ever to
tell people about the Christian message we must tell it in
language that they can understand. That is precisely what
John did.

(ii) He was giving us a new Christology. By calling Jesus
the *logos*, John said two things about Jesus. (a) Jesus *is* the
creating power of God come to men. He does not only
speak the word of *knowledge*; he *is* the word of *power*. He
did not come so much to *say* things to us, as to *do* things
for us. (b) Jesus is the incarnate mind of God. We might
well translate John's words, 'The mind of God became a

man.' A word is always 'the expression of a thought' and Jesus is the perfect expression of God's thought for men.

We should do well to rediscover and to preach again Jesus Christ as the *logos*, the *Word* of God.

MERIMNA AND MERIMNAN

THE RIGHT AND THE WRONG CARE

T H E noun *merimna* means *care, thought* or *anxiety*, and the verb *merimnan* means *to take thought for,* or *to be anxious about*. It is very important that we should correctly understand the real meaning of these two words, because the whole Christian attitude to life and to living depends on a correct understanding of them.

Both words are quite frequent in the NT. The noun *merimna* is the word that is used for the *cares of this world* which choke the life out of the good seed of the word (Matt. 13.22; cp. Mark 4.19 and Luke 8.14). It is used by Luke in the warning that the coming of Christ must not find us overcharged with surfeiting and drunkenness and *cares of this life* (Luke 21.34). It is used by Peter when he bids his friends cast all their *care* upon God (I Peter 5.7). It is used by Paul when he says that the heaviest burden of all that is upon him is the *care* of all the churches (II Cor. 11.28). We must note right at the beginning that from these uses it can be seen at once that *merimna* is a word that has a double flavour, for obviously the *cares of life* which choke the seed are not the same thing as the *care of all the churches* which was laid upon the heart of Paul.

When we turn to the verb *merimnan* we find that its most important use is in the Sermon on the Mount.

In the Sermon on the Mount it is used in Matt. 6.25, 27, 28, 31, 34; cp. Luke 12.22, 25, 26. In every case the AV translates it *to take thought for. ' Take no thought* for your life' (Matt. 6.25). 'Take no thought for the morrow' (Matt. 6.34). Now it is to be noted that the AV was the first, and is the only, version to use this translation. Wiclif translated it: 'Be not busy to your life.' Tyndale, Cranmer and the Geneva Bible all translate it: 'Be not careful of your life,' in which translation careful has it literal meaning, full of care. The RV has: 'Be not anxious for your life.' Moffatt has: 'Do not trouble about what you are to eat and drink in life.' Weymouth has: 'I charge you not to be over-anxious about your lives.' The NT in Plain English has: 'Worry no more about your life.' Rieu has: 'I bid you not to fret about your life.' The ARSV has: 'Do not be anxious about your life.' Schonfield in The Authentic New Testament has: 'Do not vex yourselves about what you are to eat or drink.' It is obvious that this is a commandment of Jesus about the meaning of which we must be clear, for it is a commandment which affects our whole attitude to life.

Before we come to discuss the meaning of it we must go on to look at the other NT uses of the word. Merimnan is used in Luke when Martha is said by Jesus to be careful about many things (Luke 10.41); and when the disciples are bidden to take no thought how they will answer the charges that will be brought against them (Luke 12.11). Merimnan is used quite frequently by Paul. He uses it several times in I Cor. 7.32-34. In that passage he is insisting that the Christian must concentrate on the Second Coming of Christ, which, at that time, he expected at any moment. The unmarried man and woman care for the things that belong to the Lord; but the married man and woman care for the things of the world, and care more how they may please each other than how they may please God. In I Cor. 12.25 merimnan is used of the care that members of the Church should have for one another. In Phil. 2.20 it is used for the care with which Timothy will concern himself for the highest interests of the Philippian church. In Phil. 4.6 Paul uses merimnan when he bids the Philippians: 'Be careful for nothing.'

It is clear again that *merimnan*, like *merimna*, has a double flavour. The *care* for our fellow Christians is obviously a different thing from the *care* for the things of this world.

We must now go on to look at the meaning of these words in secular Greek that we may better interpret their meaning in the NT.

In classical Greek *merimnan* at its simplest can simply mean *to be occupied with*. In Sophocles' play, Oedipus asks the herdsman in what labour or in what way of life he is *employed* (*merimnan*) (*Sophocles, Oedipus Tyrannus* 1124). The noun *merimna* is sometimes joined with *lupē*, which means *grief*. In Euripides' *Ion*, Ion finds Creusa weeping at the shrine and asks her: 'How cam'st thou, lady, 'neath such *load of care*?' (Euripides, *Ion* 244). The word can and docs denote real distress and trouble of mind.

In ordinary Greek the word *merimnan* can be used to describe a man thinking about his work, or a philosopher puzzling about his problems. Xenophon tells how Socrates criticised those who tried to understand the movement of the heavens and how God contrives them. He said that he who *would meddle with these matters* (*merimnan*) ran the risk of losing his sanity as completely as Anaxagoras, who took an insane pride in his explanation of divine machinery (Xenophon, *Memorabilia* 4.7.6). He tells how Socrates had no time for the theorists who *worry about* the ultimate nature of things (Xenophon, *Memorabilia* 1.1.4). He tells how Socrates said to Pericles: 'I think that *you take much trouble* (*merimnan*) that you may not unconsciously lack any knowledge useful to a general' (Xenophon, *Memorabilia* 3.5.23). In his life of Cyrus, Xenophon tells how Cyrus at the end of his days left to Tanaoxares a position of less responsibility than the kingship. It would save him from *being cumbered about with the many cares* which come from responsibility and ambition (Xenophon, *Cyropaedia* 8.7.12).

Once again we have this double meaning. Once again we can see that there is a care and an anxiety which is a right and an honourable thing; and there is a care and an anxiety which is a distracting, a distressing and an evil thing.

We now turn to our last source of information, to the contemporary Greek of the papyri. It so happens that the letters of the ordinary people in NT times quite often use the words *merimna* and *merimnan*.

A wife writes to her absent husband: 'I cannot even sleep because night and day my one *worry* (*merimna*) is your safety.' A mother, on learning that her son is well, writes: 'That is all my prayer and all my *anxiety*' (*merimna*). A soothsayer warns a client that he will be involved in many *anxieties* (*merimnai*) and distresses. Anacreon writes: 'When I drink wine my *worries* (*merimnai*) go to sleep.' In the Letter of Aristeas there is the question (271): 'What preserves a kingdom?' And the answer is: '*Care* (*merimna*) and watchfulness to see that no injury is inflicted by those who are set in positions of authority over the people.' An absent member of the family writes home: 'I am now writing in haste to prevent you being anxious (*merimnan*), for I will see to it that you are not worried.' The word *amerimnia* means *safety, security, the state of being unworried*. When two men have business dealings, the one writes to the other: 'For your *security* (*amerimnia*) I have issued to you this contract.' The contract has been drawn up and ratified so that the other partner to the deal will not worry.

So then this study of the meaning of the words *merimna* and *merimnan* in secular Greek has brought us once again to the same conclusion. There is a right and a wrong thought, a right and a wrong anxiety, a right and a wrong carefulness.

It remains now to go back to the NT and see just what that right and that wrong anxiety are. First, let us look at the wrong anxiety.

(i) The anxiety and the worry which come from too

much involvement in the affairs of the world is always wrong (Matt. 13.22; cp. Mark 4.19 and Luke 8.14; Luke 21.34). When a man gets so involved in the things of time that he has no time for the things of eternity he is in a dangerous position. When he gives so much thought and care and concentration to the things of the earth that the things of heaven are crowded out he is in a perilous situation. A man may be so much with men that he has no time to be with God. He may have so many words to say to men that he has no time to pray to God. Be it noted, his engagement in the world may be with things which in themselves are not bad things, but 'the second best can often be the worst enemy of the best'.

(ii) Worry about the future is always wrong. It is wrong because it is *blind*; it fails to see God's bounty in the world; if God cares for the birds and the flowers, surely he will care for men (Matt. 6.25, 26, 28-30). It is wrong because it is *useless*. Worry never achieved anything (Matt. 6.27). It is wrong because it is essentially *irreligious* (Matt. 6.32). A Gentile may worry, but not a Christian. It is wrong because it merely *incapacitates a man from meeting problems when they do come* (Matt. 6.34). Worry does not make a man more able to face a situation; it makes him less able to face it.

(iii) Worry is wrong when it means the expenditure of energy on non-essentials. That was why Martha was wrong (Luke 10.41). It was not a big meal Jesus wanted; it was peace before the Cross.

(iv) Worry about how to face the oppositions and the trials which come to a Christian is wrong (Luke 12.11). With the need there will come the power. God does not let down the man who is true to him.

(v) Worry about how to please the wrong people is wrong (I Cor. 7.32-34). It is not men whom we seek to please; it is God. And if a man fears God enough, he will never fear the face of any man.

(vi) The cure for worry is to cast oneself and all things

upon God (I Peter 5.7; Phil. 4.6). In other words, the cure for worry is the realization that we are not left to handle life alone; we face it with God.

Second, let us look at the right kind of anxiety.

(i) It is right that we should take thought for *each other* (I Cor. 12.25). It may in fact often happen that the best way to forget our own worries is to shoulder someone else's. Life becomes an easier and a bigger thing when we feel the troubles of others more than we feel our own.

(ii) It is specially right to take thought for our fellow-Christians (Phil. 2.20). Timothy was the man who would take all thought for the needs of the Philippians. No Christian can be a happy when other Christians, of any colour or of any country, are in distress and persecution and need.

(iii) It is right to take thought for the Church of Christ (II Cor. 11.28). Paul's care for all the churches was at once his burden and his privilege. The Christian will ever think and plan how best he may serve his church.

It is true that we are told to take no thought for life and the morrow. But what is forbidden is disabling worry and not enabling foresight. It is the duty of a Christian man to do all that he can and to dare all that he can and to leave the rest to God. And at the same time it is the duty of a Christian man to have the same care and the same thought and the same anxiety for his fellow men, his fellow-Christians, and his church, as God himself has.

PARAGGELIA AND PARAGGELLEIN

THE WORDS OF COMMAND

PARAGGELIA and *paraggellein* are characteristically words of command. *Paraggelia* is a noun which means *an order, an instruction, a charge, a command;* and *paraggellein* is a verb which means *to charge, to instruct, to give* or *to pass on an order.* The great interest of these words lies

in the background against which they are used. They have
five different areas and spheres within which they are used.

(i) First and foremost, they are *military* words. *Paraggelia* is distinctively *a command issued to soldiers*. *Paraggellein* is distinctively the word used of *a general issuing a word of command*, and of that word of command being passed from commander to commander, from rank to rank and from man to man.

Xenophon tells how in battle Cyrus armed himself, and *passed the word to others* to do the same (Xenophon, *Anabasis* 1.8.3). He tells how on the occasion of a ceremonial parade Cyrus gave an *order* to his first captain to take up his position at the head of the line, and *to transmit the same order* to the second captain, and so on (Xenophon, *Cyropaedia* 2.4.2). He tells how the officers were to bid the corporals each one *to announce* it to his squad (Xenophon, *Cyropaedia* 4.2.7). *Paraggelia* and *paraggellein* are characteristically words of military command.

(ii) They are *legal words*. They are the words which are used of summoning a man to court, or of citing him to appear in a certain place that he may give account for the things that he has done, or of laying certain legal injunctions upon him, which he must satisfy and obey.

In the papyri one man writes to another to tell him that, now that he has received the written *paraggelia*, instruction, he must take thought for the cultivation of his fields. The warning is issued that if certain people disobey this *paraggelia*, injunction, they will pay the penalty of their disobedience. An official is directed to serve warning upon a man, so that he may have a written *summons* to appear wherever the prefect shall hold his court. An official is instructed to give *written notice* to a man who is arraigned for murder and other crimes to appear before the court in three days' time.

The words develop a general sense of giving instructions or injunctions to a person. For instance, *paraggellein* is used in the papyri of ordering someone out of the house, of telling a person to go to a certain street, of giving notice of a certain obligation. The legal and the military sense meet in the kindred word *paraggelma*, which can be used for a *mobilization order*.

(iii) They are *ethical* words. They are used of the instructions that the ethical teacher gives to his disciples. Clement of Rome writes of God: 'He who has *ordered* us not to lie, how much more will he not lie himself' (I *Clement* 27.2).

When Aristotle is talking about individual judgments on individual people, he says that they cannot be dealt with by rule, because there is no science and no set of *rules* which can be used (Aristotle, *Nicomachean Ethics* 1104a 7). The ethical rules of life are *paraggeliai*.

(iv) They are words of *technique*. The rules of grammar, the rules of literary composition or of oratory are *paraggeliai* or *paraggelmata*. Longinus insists that there are rules for great art, and he writes: 'First of all, we must raise the question whether there is such a thing as an art of the sublime or the lofty. Some hold that those are entirely in error who would bring such matters under *the precepts of art, paraggelmata*' (Longinus, *On the Sublime* 2.1). These words describe the laws and the rules of any technique or of any art.

(v) They are *medical* words. *Paraggellein* is the word that is used of a doctor *prescribing* for a case. They describe the instructions which a man must obey if he is to enjoy or to recover his health.

Now we must turn to the use of these words in the NT itself.

Within the NT itself the word *paraggelia* is used five times. In Acts 5.28 it is used of the command of the Sanhedrin to Peter and John not to preach or to teach in the name of Jesus. In Acts 16.24 it is used of the magistrates' command to the Philippian gaoler to keep Paul and Silas secure in prison. In I Thess. 4.2 it is used of the instructions which Paul gave to the church at Thessalonica. And in I Tim. 1.5 and 1.18 it is used of Paul's instructions to Timothy.

The verb *paraggellein* is much more frequently used. In the Synoptic Gospels, in Matt. 10.5 and Mark 6.8, it is used of the commands of Jesus to his disciples before he sent them out on their mission of preaching and teaching and healing. These commandments are, as it were, Jesus' marching orders to his men. In modern language, they are being briefed for the expedition on which they are being sent.

Similarly, in Acts 1.4 it is used of Jesus' command to his disciples to wait in Jerusalem until the Holy Spirit should come upon them. In Matt. 15.35 and Mark 8.6 it is used of Jesus' command to the crowd to sit upon the grass before the feeding of the five thousand.

In Luke 5.14 it is used of Jesus' instructions to the leper after he had healed him. In Luke 8.29 it is used of Jesus' command to the evil spirit to come out of the Gerasene demoniac. In Luke 8.56 it is used of Jesus' instruction to Jairus and his wife not to talk of the miracle of the raising of their daughter.

In Luke 9.21 it is used of Jesus' command to his disciples not yet to spread abroad their discovery that he was the Christ. The notable thing is that in the Synoptic Gospels the verb *paraggellein* is never used of anyone except Jesus. It is the characteristic word for his instructions to his people.

We now look at the word in the rest of the NT. It occurs sometimes in its normal secular use of the command issued by a higher authority to a subordinate. In Acts 4.18; 5.28, 40 it is used of the command of the Sanhedrin to Peter and John to stop preaching. In Acts 15.5 it is used of the command of the Pharisees to observe the ceremonial law. In Acts 16.23 it is used of the command of the Philippian magistrates that Paul and Silas should be thrown into prison. In Acts 23.22, 30 it is used of the instructions of the Roman captain to the young man who had given him information regarding the plot to assassinate Paul. All these usages are the normal secular usages. They are all commands of the military or the civil authority.

But the word becomes of great interest when we examine its remaining uses. We discover that it is the regular word for Christian instruction, and that it is the word which is uniquely characteristic of the commands and the instructions and the training which Paul gave to his friends and converts.

It is used of Paul's command to the evil spirit to come out of the Philippian slave girl in Acts 16.18. In I Cor. 7.10 it is used of Paul's insistence that the marriage bond is not to be broken, a command which he says comes from the Lord. In I Cor. 11.17 it is used of Paul's instructions to the Corinthian church regarding the Lord's Supper. In I Thess. 4.11 it is used of Paul's command to the Thessalonians to be quiet and to mind their own business. In II Thess. 3.4, 6, 10, 12 it is used of a whole series of commandments of Paul to the Thessalonian church.

Paraggellein is a word which is almost characteristic of the Pastoral Epistles. It is used of the instructions given to Timothy in I Tim. 1.3; of the work which Timothy must do, that he must *command* and teach these things (I Tim. 4.11); of the charge which is to be made to the widows concerning how they must live (I Tim. 5.7); of the solemn charge to Timothy to keep the commandments (I Tim. 6.13); and of the charge to the rich not to be proud because of their riches (I Tim. 6.17).

We have now reached the most interesting and significant fact that *paraggellein* is the characteristic word for the commandments of Jesus to his people, and for the instruction of Paul to his converts in the early Church. We must now go on to see what the significance of that fact is for the Christian life.

The very fact that these words are so often and so consistently used tells us certain things about the Christian and about the Christian life. We have seen that these words have five backgrounds, five areas and spheres which define their use.

(i) They are the words of *military command*. The Christian must regard himself as a soldier; he must regard himself as a man under orders; he must regard himself as a man having a definite commission; he must regard himself as a man on a campaign.

The Christian must therefore see himself, not as a man who is in the world to do as he likes, but as a man who is in the world to do as his commander orders. Further, the Christian must not see himself as an individual, but as a member of an army, a unit in the task-force of Jesus Christ. Too much independence and too much individualism are alike forbidden by these words.

(ii) They are the words of *legal summons*. The Christian must regard himself as a man under responsibility; he must regard himself as a man who is answerable for all that he does. The Christian is a man under judgment. His life must be aimed not to satisfy himself, not to please his fellow-men, but to stand the scrutiny of God.

(iii) They are the words of *the ethical teacher*. The Christian must regard himself as a man under instruction and discipline, as a man learning the laws and the rules of life. The foolish man is the man who thinks that he knows it all already; the wisest man is the man who knows that he does not know.

The Christian will be invited to direct his life by many standards, the standards of business practices, the standards of worldly wisdom, the standards of human cleverness; his one standard must be the teaching of Jesus Christ.

(iv) They are the words of *instruction in technique*. The Christian has not only to learn a series of ethical laws; he has to learn the art of living the Christian life. His study is not confined to the class-room or the library or the discussion circle or the prayer group. He is under the obligation, not only to learn, but also to live Christianity. He is learning, not only a theology for thought, but also a technique for living.

In *Prayers for the Lambeth Conference of 1948* there is this prayer: 'Almighty God, give us grace to be not only

hearers but doers of thy holy word, not only to admire but
to obey thy doctrine, not only to profess but to practise
thy religion, not only to love but to live thy gospel. So grant
that what we learn of thy glory we may receive into our
hearts and show forth in our lives, through Jesus Christ
our Lord.'

Therein is summed up the Christian duty. Technique may
nowadays be a word which is belittled, but there is not
only a theology but also a technique of the Christian life.

(v) They are the words of *medical treatment*. Epictetus
called his lecture-room 'the hospital of the sick soul'. He
called his teaching 'the medicines of salvation'. Men are
sick in soul and must come to Jesus Christ for healing. No
doctor can heal any man unless that man submits to the
doctor's treatment, accepts the doctor's prescription, and
obeys the doctor's instructions. The Christian is the man
who has realized the sickness of his soul, who has come to
Christ for a cure, and who is determined to submit his life
to the treatment which Christ prescribes.

So these words *paraggelia* and *paraggellein* tell us that the
Christian is the soldier of Christ, the man on trial before
Christ, the disciple of Christ, the trainee of Christ and the
patient of Christ.

PARAKLĒTOS

THE WORD OF THE HOLY SPIRIT

PARAKLĒTOS is one of the great characteristic words of
the Johannine writings. In the Fourth Gospel it is used as a
title of the Holy Spirit in 14.16; 14.26; 15.26; 16.7; and in
the First Epistle it is used of Jesus as the advocate who
pleads our cause with the Father (I John 2.1). Clearly it is a
word of quite special importance; but when we look at the
efforts of translators to render it into English, equally

clearly it is a word of quite special difficulty. In the passage
in the First Epistle the translators are almost unanimous in
rendering *paraklētos* by the word *advocate*. The only
exception is the Twentieth Century New Testament, which
renders it *one who pleads our cause*, which is simply a
description of the work which an advocate does. But in the
Fourth Gospel itself the translations are many and varied.
The AV translates it *comforter*; the RV retains the word
comforter, but in the margin gives *advocate* and *helper* and
notes that the Greek is *paraclete*. The ARSV translates it
counsellor. J. B. Phillips translates it *someone to stand by
you*. Ronald Knox translates it *he who is to befriend you*.
Moffatt, Torrey and the Twentieth Century New Testament
all translate it *helper*. Clearly this is a difficult word to
translate. We shall come to see that the difficulty lies in the
fact that the word means so much that there is no single
English word by which it can be adequately translated.

The English translation *comforter* goes all the way back
to Wiclif; but it must be noted that Wiclif was using the
word *comforter* with a width of meaning which in modern
English it does not possess. The proof of this is that Wiclif
translates Eph. 6.10, 'Be ye *comforted* in the Lord.' The
word there is *endunamoun*, which has in it the same root as
the root of the word *dunamis*, which means *power*, and
which is the word from which the English word *dynamite*
is derived. In point of fact Tyndale translated Eph. 6.10,
'Be strong in the Lord,' a translation which has survived
down to the present day. This same word, *endunamoun*,
is used in I Tim. 1.12 where once again Wiclif translates,
'I do thankings to him that *comforted* me.' Tyndale has,
'I thank him who has *made me strong*,' and the AV has,
'I thank him who hath *enabled* me.' In modern English the
word *comforter* has to do exclusively with comfort and
consolation and sympathy in sorrow and in distress; but in
Wiclif's time it was much more closely connected with its
root, the Latin word *fortis*, which means, *brave, strong,
courageous*. So we may note to begin with that when Wiclif

translated *paraklētos* by the word *comforter* he was certainly not saying that the sole, or even the main, function
of the Holy Spirit was to comfort and console in our sense
of the words; he was meaning that the function of the
Holy Spirit was to fill a man with that Spirit of power and
courage which would make him able triumphantly to cope
with life. It is in fact a great misfortune that the narrowing
of the word *comforter* has resulted in an undue narrowing
of our conception of the work of the Holy Spirit.

It is again to be noted that even the early Fathers have
difficulty with the word *paraklētos*. Origen would translate
it *consoler* in the Gospel and *advocate* in the Epistle. Cyril
of Jerusalem would translate it *consoler*, because the Spirit
helps our infirmities and makes intercession for us. Hilary
and Jerome both translate it *consolator*, again stressing the
idea of *consolation*. Tertullian varies. Sometimes he merely
transliterates into *paracletus*; sometimes he has *advocatus*,
an advocate to plead our cause; and once he has the very
unusual word *exorator* which means a *successful suppliant*,
one who obtains by entreaty.

Let us then see if we can come at something of the riches
of the meaning of this word.

Paraklētos itself is a word which is passive in form. It
means literally *one who is called in*. But although it is
passive in form it is almost always *active in meaning*,
because the thing that gives it its meaning is the purpose
and the function for which the person is called in. He is
always called in in order that he may do something, that he
may render some service. Therefore the word is a word
with a *passive form* but an *active meaning*.

If that be so we shall come best at its meaning by
examining first of all the verb *parakalein* from which
paraklētos is derived.

(i) At its most general *parakalein* means *to call in, to
summon*. So a man is said to call in an *ally* (*summachos*)
(Herodotus, 7.158); to call in a *counsellor* to give advice
(*sumboulos*) (Xenophon, *Anabasis* 1.6.5); to call in an *advo-*

cate to plead a case in the law courts (*sunēgoros*) (Aeschines, 2.184). It is also used of calling upon a man *to undertake a public duty* such as the duty of gymnasiarch, whose duty it was to maintain and train a team at his own expense to run in the torch race. Finally, it is used of calling in the gods as *helpers* (*boēthoi*) (Epictetus, 3.21.12). It is clear that in every case the summons is to help, to service, to assistance. Therefore at its widest a *paraklētos* is a person who is called in to help in a situation with which a man by himself cannot cope. It is true that the basic meaning of *paraklētos* is *helper*, but we must now try to put some more definite content into the meaning of the help which is sought and given.

(ii) Let us look next at one of the rare meanings of the word *parakalein*. In ordinary secular Greek the word *parakalein* very rarely means to *comfort*, in the sense of to *console*. But it does have that meaning in the Septuagint. It is so used in Ps. 71.21, 'Thou shalt increase my greatness and *comfort* me on every side.' It is the word which is used in the great passage in Isa. 40.1, 2, '*Comfort* ye, *comfort* ye my people, saith your God.' In the two later versions of the Septuagint, those of Aquila and Theodotion, *paraklētos* is the word used in Job 16.2, 'Miserable *comforters* are ye all.' It is then possible to take *paraklētos* to mean *one called in to comfort and to console*; but two things have to be noted. First, it is by far the rarest meaning of the word. Second, even if it be taken in that sense, it still has the background of a comfort which makes a man able to stand on his two feet and face life. In Job 4.4 the Moffatt translation is, 'Your words have kept men on their feet,' and that is a description of the effect of the comfort which *parakalein* describes.

(iii) In ordinary secular Greek by far the most characteristic usage both of *parakalein* and *paraklētos* is in connection with help given in some kind of legal trial. In Greece the *paraklētos* was the friend of the accused person, called in to speak in support of his character, in order to enlist the sympathy of the judges in his favour. In Demosthenes it can be used for the counsel for the defence. It means someone who will present someone else's case to some other person or to some other authority in the most favourable light. Diogenes Laertius (4.50) tells about the answer of the philosopher Bion to a man who was a talkative nuisance. Bion said: 'I will do my best for you if you send *paraklētoi, representatives*, to plead your case, and if you don't come yourself.' The *paraklētoi* would put a much more effective case than the man himself. Philo (*In Flaccum* 4) tells how the Alexandrian Jews wished to find someone to plead their case with the Roman Emperor; they in fact wished the city of Alexandria to plead it for them. He says: 'We must find a more powerful *paraklētos, advocate*, by whom Gaius will be brought to a favourable disposition towards us.' The *Epistle of Barnabas* (20) speaks of those who are *paraklētoi, advocates*, of the wealthy and the unjust, and accusers of the poor. Philo (*De Josepho* 40) tells of the answer of Joseph to his brethren when they were in obvious terror that he would revenge himself upon them, 'I grant you free forgiveness for all that you have done to me; you need no one else to intercede for you, no other *paraklētos*.' Philo speaks of God himself creating and blessing the world (*De Mund. Opif.*), 'employing not any *paraklētos, adviser, helper*—for who else was there—but only himself, did God resolve that he ought to bless the world with his benefits.' The *Second Letter of Clement* (6) says: 'Who will be our *paraklētos* if we are found doing that which is not right?' That is to say: 'Who will speak for us, plead for us, take up our cause against the justice of God?' In the Letter of the Churches of Lyons and Vienne (quoted in Eusebius, *Ecclesiastical History*, 5.1) when certain of the Christians were on trial for their faith, Vettius Epagathus, one of the Roman officials, himself confessed to being Christian, and was thereupon called the *paraklētos* of the Christians, the advocate of the Christian cause.

This usage of the word became transliterated into later Jewish language. The Targum, that is the authorized translation, of Job 33.23 says that in order to redeem man from going down into the pit, a special angelic agency, a mediator, an interpreter, a *paraklētos* is necessary.

The later Rabbis wrote the word *paraklētos* in Hebrew letters and used it quite freely. 'He who fulfils one precept of the Law gains for himself one *paraklētos*, *advocate*; he who commits one transgression gains to himself one *katēgoros*, *accuser*.' 'In the heavenly judgment a man's *paraklētoi*, *advocates*, are repentance and good works.' 'All the righteousness and mercy which an Israelite doeth in the world, are great peace and great *paraklētoi*, *advocates*, between him and his Father in heaven.'

There is no doubt that this is the meaning of *paraklētos* in I John 2.1. Jesus is the prisoner's friend. He is the one who will plead our cause. He is the one who will plead and intercede for us. He is the counsel for the defence. The Jew had the hopeless task of putting forward as his defence before God his own good works and his own obedience to the Law. The Christian has the supreme defence—the advocacy of Jesus Christ himself. It is he who ever liveth to make intercession for us.

(iv) The meaning of advocate for the defence is both fitting and adequate for *paraklētos* in I John 2.1; but it is not so fitting in the Gospel. There the *paraklētos* is the Spirit of truth (14.16); there the Spirit is the interpreter and the teacher and the remembrancer (14.26); there the Spirit is the one who will testify of Christ (15.26); there the Spirit comes when Jesus goes away (16.7). In the Gospel, as Dr. G. H. C. Macgregor finely puts it, the Spirit is Christ's *alter ego*. The *paraklētos*, the Spirit, is the constant, illuminating, strengthening, enabling presence of Jesus. Now it so happens that there is still another meaning of *parakalein* which will give us the key. *Parakalein* not infrequently means to *exhort* or *to urge*. It is used by Xenophon for exhorting men to the fairest deeds (*Anabasis* 3.1.24). It is used by Plato for exhorting men to apply their minds to think about things (*Republic* 535b); it is used by Isocrates of urging men to remember (3.12). It is fairly frequently used of inciting a person to a certain action or emotion.

But above all *parakalein* is used of *exhorting troops who are about to go into battle*. Aeschylus (*Persae* 380) says of the ships sailing into battle; 'The long galleys cheered (*parakalein*) each other, line by line.' Euripides (*Phoenissae* 1254) describing the plans for battle says : 'So did they hail them, *cheering* them to fight.' Xenophon uses it of urging the soldiers to embark upon the ships and to set out on an adventurous voyage (*Anabasis* 5.6.19). Polybius uses it of Lutatius addressing his troops before a naval battle with the Carthaginians (1.60.5). He uses it of Demetrius rallying his men and addressing the ranks before they embarked upon battle (3.19.4). And the word he uses of embarking upon battle is *diakinduneuein*, which means *to accept the risk of battle*.

Again and again we find that *parakalein* is *the word of the rallying-call*; it is the word used of the speeches of leaders and of soldiers who urge each other on. It is the word used of words which send fearful and timorous and hesitant soldiers and sailors courageously into battle. A *paraklētos* is therefore an *encourager*, one who puts courage into the faint-hearted, one who nerves the feeble arm for fight, one who makes a very ordinary man cope gallantly with a perilous and a dangerous situation.

Here then we have the great work of the Holy Spirit. To put it in modern language, the Holy Spirit makes men able to cope with life. The Holy Spirit is in fact the fulfilment of the promise, 'Lo, I am with you always even unto the end of the world' (Matt. 28.20).

It is quite clear that the translation *comforter* which in the days of Wiclif was perfectly adequate and correct for *paraklētos* has now become much too narrow and much too limited. To limit, even by suggestion, the work of the Holy Spirit to consolation and to comfort is sadly to belittle the work of the Spirit. By the study of the word *paraklētos* we have come to see the wide scope in time and eternity of the *paraklētos*.

(i) The word *paraklētos* always means someone called into help and to render some service; therefore the Holy Spirit is essentially the helper of men.

(ii) The word *paraklētos* has a great Septuagint background of that kind of comfort and consolation in distress which keeps a man on his feet, when, left to himself, he would collapse. It is the comfort which enables a man to pass the breaking-point and not to break.

(iii) The word *paraklētos* has a great background in Greek law. The *paraklētos* was the prisoner's friend, the advocate and counsel for the defence, the man who bore witness to his friend's character when he most needed it, and when others wished to condemn him; therefore when we describe the glorified Christ as our *paraklētos* we mean that he is there to speak for us before God.

(iv) The word *parakalein* is the word for exhorting men to noble deeds and high thoughts; it is especially the word of courage before battle. Life is always calling us into battle and the one who makes us able to stand up to the opposing forces, to cope with life and to conquer life is the *paraklētos*, the Holy Spirit, who is none other than the presence and the power of the risen Christ.

PENTHEIN

THE WORD OF GODLY SORROW

PENTHEIN, the verb which means *to sorrow*, is by no means an unusual Greek word. In the NT it occurs nine times.

Jesus said that was not possible that the friends of the bridegroom should *mourn* while the bridegroom was still with them (Matt. 9.15). Paul rebukes the Corinthian church because its members did not *mourn* for the man whose sin had shamed the church (I Cor. 5.2). Paul's fear is that he will have cause *to bewail* the sinners, if he comes again to Corinth (II Cor. 12.21). In James the sinners are invited to return to God, and to be afflicted, *to mourn*, and to weep (James 4.9). Three times in the Revelation the word is used of the *mourning* which shall follow the destruction of the great Babylon (Rev. 18.11, 15, 19).

But the most important use of this word is in the Beatitudes. Luke has it: Woe to you that laugh now! For ye shall *mourn* and weep (Luke 6.25). And Matthew has it: Blessed are they that *mourn* for they shall be comforted (Matt. 5.4).

There are two most significant things about this word.

(i) *Penthein* is the strongest word for mourning in the Greek language. It is the word which in all ages of Greek is used for mourning for the dead, or for one who is as if he were dead. So it is used in Homer (*Iliad* 19.225) and in Herodotus (4.95). So Sophocles speaks of Oedipus shaken with the spasms of *agonizing* memory (Sophocles, *Oedipus Tyrannus* 1320).

In the Septuagint it is the word which is used for Jacob's *mourning* when he thinks that Joseph is dead and gone for ever (Gen. 37.34); and it is the word which is used for David's *mourning* when his son Absalom met his tragic death (II Sam. 19.1).

In the papyri again it is connected with the *mourning* of death and of unbridgeable separation. In one papyrus it is laid down: The *mourning* women shall wear dark raiment. In another a husband who is separated from his wife writes: I wish you to know that ever since you left me I have been in *mourning*, weeping by night, and *mourning* by day.

There is no stronger word of mourning in the Greek language than *penthein*.

(ii) It must have been noticed in the examples quoted

how often *mourning* and *weeping* (*penthein* and *klaiein*) are associated. The second significant fact about *penthein* is that it described *the mourning which cannot be hidden*.

It describes, not only a grief which brings an ache to the heart, but also a grief which brings tears to the eyes. *Penthein* describes the sorrow which cannot be concealed.

This then is the word which the NT uses for a Christian's *mourning for his sin* (Matt. 5.4; I Cor. 5.2; II Cor. 12.21; James 4.9). The Christian sorrow for sin must be not only a gentle, vague, sentimental regret that something has gone wrong; it must be a sorrow as acute as sorrow for the dead.

It must be a sorrow which is not hidden, but which emerges in the tears and the confession of the truly penitent heart. It is a sorrow which realizes what Carlyle called 'the infinite damnability of sin', and which is broken in heart when in the Cross it sees what sin can do.

One of the great conversion stories of modern times is the story of how the Japanese murderer Tokichi Ishii was converted by reading the NT when he was in prison. He was a man of the most savage cruelty, bestial and sub-human in the terrible crimes that he had committed.

He was converted by reading a Bible which two Canadian women left with him, when they could not get even a flicker of human response to anything they said to him. He read it, and when he came to the prayer of Jesus: 'Father, forgive them, they know not what they do,' he says: 'I stopped. I was stabbed to the heart, as if pierced with a five-inch nail.' His sorrow for his sin was the sorrow of a broken heart.

The word *penthein* tells us that we have not even begun on the Christian way until we take sin with such seriousness that our sorrow for it is like the mourning of one who mourns for the dead. Christianity begins with the godly sorrow of the broken heart.

POIKILOS

THE MANY-COLOURED WORD

THE word *poikilos* is not in itself one of the great NT words. For the most part its usage in the NT requires no comment; but *poikilos* is worth studying for one single NT occurrence of it.

In secular Greek *poikilos* basically means *many-coloured*. It is frequently so used of natural objects. A leopard skin is said to be *poikilos*, many-coloured. A snake is said to be *poikilos*; the word describes the iridescent quality of the snake's skin. The plumage of birds is said to be *poikilos*; the word describes the many-coloured sheen of the feathers. Red granite stone is said to be *poikilos*; the word describes the many-coloured glint of the granite as the light strikes upon it.

Poikilos goes on to describe, not only natural objects, but things made and manufactured by the hands of men. It means *wrought in various colours, cunningly made*. So, in describing cloth, it is the opposite of self-coloured. It describes a many-coloured carpet; it describes a richly embroidered robe of many colours. It describes the cunningly-wrought metal work of an elaborately embossed shield.

Poikilos goes a step further. It describes anything which is *intricate* or *complex*. So it can describe an elaborately compounded medicine, or a complex and complicated law. From this it goes on to describe a person who is subtle, artful, wily, resourceful to meet any occasion or any emergency.

In this sense it can even descend to a rather bad meaning, and it can describe a person who is too clever and too subtle, a person full of tricks and stratagems to further his own ends and to get his own way.

It can be seen that in secular Greek *poikilos* is a vivid and a many-coloured word.

As we have said, in the NT the great majority of the cases where it occurs have no particular interest. It is the word which the AV commonly translates *divers*. Jesus healed those who were sick of *divers, poikilos,* diseases (Matt. 4.24; Mark 1.34; Luke 4.40). The Pastoral Epistles speak of silly women, led away with *divers, poikilos,* lusts (II Tim. 3.6); and of the *divers* lusts and pleasures characteristic of the heathen life (Titus 3.3).

The writer to the Hebrews speaks of *divers* miracles of God (Heb. 2.4); and of *divers* and strange doctrines (Heb. 13.9). James speaks of *divers* temptations (James 1.2); and Peter uses the same phrase, but the AV in his case translates it *manifold* temptations (I Peter 1.6).

But there is one occasion on which Peter, with a touch of sheer genius, uses this word *poikilos* to describe *the grace of God*. The AV translates it the *manifold* grace of God (I Peter 4.10). When we remember what *poikilos* means, this is a tremendous thought.

(i) *Poikilos* means *many-coloured*; therefore to speak of the grace of God as *poikilos* means that there is no colour in the human situation which the grace of God cannot match. It matters not whether a man is living in the gold of the sunshine of joy or success, or in the sombre black of sorrow and pain, there is that in the grace of God which can match his situation. No possible situation can arise in life which the grace of God cannot match and answer. The grace of God is a many-coloured thing with that in it which can match and meet every possible situation in life.

(ii) *Poikilos* means *artful, clever, resourceful*; therefore to speak of the grace of God as *poikilos* means that no possible problem can arise to which the grace of God cannot supply the solution; no possible task can be laid upon us which the grace of God cannot find a way to do. There is no possible set of circumstances, no possible crisis, emergency or demand through which the grace of God cannot find a way, and which the grace of God cannot triumphantly deal with and overcome. There is nothing in life with which the grace of God cannot cope.

This vivid word *poikilos* leads our thoughts straight to that many-coloured grace of God which is indeed sufficient for all things.

SEMNOS AND SEMNOTĒS

THE MAJESTY OF THE CHRISTIAN LIFE

THE adjective *semnos* and the noun *semnotēs* are characteristic words of the Pastoral Epistles. Only once does *semnos* occur outside the Pastoral Epistles. It is used in Phil. 4.8 in the phrase 'whatsoever things are *honest*'.

In the Pastoral Epistles *semnos* occurs three times. The deacons must be *grave* (I Tim. 3.8); the women, or perhaps it should be translated their wives, should have the same quality (I Tim. 3.11). The aged women must live *as becometh holiness* (Titus 2.3).

The noun *semnotēs* also occurs three times in the Pastoral Epistles. Prayer is to be made for kings and those in authority that we may live a quiet and peaceable life in all godliness and in all *honesty* (I Tim. 2.2). *Semnotēs, gravity,* is the quality which should be the outstanding quality of a good father (I Tim. 3.4), and of a good teacher (Titus 2.7).

Clearly this quality of *gravity* and *dignity* was meant to be the characteristic of the Christian life.

These words have a most notable background and atmosphere in secular Greek. It may truly be said that there are no more majestic words in the whole Greek language. Let us study their usage in ordinary Greek that we may see just what they demand of the Christian, and that we may understand the quality in which the Christian life is to be clothed.

(i) The word *semnos* is particularly connected with the gods. It means *revered, august, holy*. Apollo is called by Aeschylus *the august commander* (*The Seven against Thebes* 800). Poseidon is called *awful Poseidon* by Sophocles (*Oedipus Coloneus 55*).

The sacrifices of the gods are *holy* sacrifices (Pindar, *Olymp.* 7.42); the temple of Apollo is a *holy* house (Pindar, *Nem.* 1.72). In every case the word used is *semnos*, for *semnos* is a word with the majesty of divinity in it.

(ii) But there were certain gods of whom this word was specially used. It was specially used of the Erinyes, the Furies whose duty and task it was to avenge sin. So much so was this the case that these Furies were actually called the *semnai* (the feminine plural of the adjective). There were three of these grim goddesses, Allecto, 'she who never rests', Tisiphone, 'the avenger of murder', and Megaera, 'the jealous one', and once a man had sinned they were on his heels, and neither in this world or the next did they let him go. 'They are the avengers of every transgression of natural order, and especially of offences which touch the foundation of human society. They punish, without mercy, all violations of filial duty, or the claims of kinship, or the rites of hospitality; murder, perjury and like offences. . . . The punishment begins on earth and is continued after death.' The Erinyes, the Furies, the *semnai* were nothing less than the custodians of divine justice. There is much about them in Greek tragedy. Sophocles calls them '*majestic* swift-footed hounds of vengeance' (*Ajax* 837).

Euripides says of them: 'They are the *dread* ones; wise art thou to name them not.' The most terrible description of the *semnai* is in Aeschylus' play, *The Eumenides*. *Eumenides* means *The Gracious Ones*, and the Greeks called the Erinyes, the Furies, by that name in order to please them and to avert their wrath. There the chorus of the avengers says: 'No wrath from us creeps up on him who has clean hands, but unharmed he passes the age of his life; but whosoever sins, as this man has done, and seeks to hide the hands in murder dipped, to him we appear, true witnesses to the dead, come as the avengers of blood, avengers who cannot fail in their task' (Aeschylus, *The Eumenides* 313-320).

There is all the majesty of the divine in this word *semnos*, and it is the word which describes the characteristic quality of the Christian.

But these words have still other and illuminating uses.

(i) They are words which have to do with *royalty* and with *kingliness*. Herodotus tells how the Egyptians disapproved of the lax and drunken conduct of their king, and how they said: 'We would have you sit aloft upon a throne *of pride*' (Herodotus, 2.173). Euripides speaks of a '*proud* despot' (*The Suppliant Women* 384). Plato uses *semnos* to describe the 'most *important* and influential men in our cities' (Plato, *Phaedrus* 257d).

Aristophanes in his skit *The Ecclesiazusae*, in which the women take over the government and wipe out social distinctions, says, as Rogers translates it into English verse:

'By the side of the beauty so *stately and grand*
    The dwarf, the deformed and the ugly shall stand.'

Xenophon uses the word *semnotēs* to describe the *magnificence* of the appearance of Cyrus, the Persian king, as he drove forth in state. *Semnos* and *semnotēs* have in them all the majesty of kingship and of royalty.

(ii) They are words which are very commonly used to express that which is *stately* and *dignified* in language and in expression. Aristotle says that the metre of poetry which was called the heroic metre is *semnos*, dignified (Aristotle, *Rhetoric* 1408b 35).

Plato speaks of *stately* and wonderful tragic poetry (Plato, *Gorgias* 502b). Pindar speaks of untruths which are dressed in great language, and says, 'His falsehoods through winged artifice wear a flower of *dignity*' (Pindar, *Nem.* 7.22).

Herodotus speaks of using *high* language in the presence of a king (Herodotus, 7.6).

When Aristotle is discussing literary style, he writes: 'The merit of diction is to be clear without being commonplace. The clearest diction is that made up of ordinary words, but it is commonplace. . . . That which employs unfamiliar words is *dignified*, *semnos* and outside the common usage' (Aristotle, *Poetics* 1458a 21). Once again we come to this idea of solemnity and of dignity and of gravity and of weight.

(iii) Still another use of *semnos* and *semnotēs* is that they occur very frequently on sepulchral inscriptions. They are favourite words used in describing and paying tribute to those who have lived well and nobly and who are gone to their rest. Here then is still another great series of meanings which these words possess. Here is another atmosphere in which they moved.

They are used to express all the majesty of royalty and of kingship.

They are used to express all the weight and the dignity and the solemnity of speech at its highest and its best and its most moving. They are used to express all that is lovely and all that demands respect in life. No greater tribute can be paid to one who has passed on than to say he was *semnos* and lived with *semnotēs*, that on his life there was the royal dignity and the kingly majesty of goodness.

Aristotle, the greatest of the Greek ethical writers, and one of the great ethical teachers of all time, has much to say about the man who is *semnos* and the quality of *semnotēs*.

In the *Nicomachean Ethics* he talks of 'the great-souled man'. He says that it is characteristic of such a man 'never to ask help from others, or only with reluctance, but to render aid willingly; and to be haughty towards men of position and fortune, but courteous towards those of moderate station, because it is difficult and *distinguished* (*semnos*) to be superior to the great, but easy to outdo the lowly, and *to adopt a high manner* (*semnunesthai*, the verb from *semnos*) with the former is not ill-bred, but it is vulgar to lord it over humble people' (*Nicomachean Ethics* 1124b 21). The man who is *semnos* knows the time for dignity.

Aristotle says that if a man's desires are weak and not evil in any event, there is nothing *to be proud of* (*semnos*) in resisting them (*ibid.* 1146a 15).

Aristotle had a habit of defining every virtue as the mean, the happy medium, between two extremes. On the one hand there is an extreme of excess of a quality, on the other hand there is the extreme of defect of a quality, and in the middle there is the happy medium. So Aristotle defines that which is *semnos* as the mean between *areskeia* and *authadia*. *Areskeia* is the characteristic of the man who is so eager to please that he is like a fawning dog; *authadia* is the characteristic of the man who thinks so little of pleasing that he is like an ill-mannered boor. *Semnos* is the word which describes the man who carries himself towards other men with a combination of dignified independence and kindly consideration. He is the man who, as Aristotle said, is 'kindly and lovely in his gravity' (Aristotle, *Rhetoric* 1391a 28). He said that the man who was *semnos* was the man who was dignified without being heavily pompous.

When Plutarch was describing the great commander Nicias, he said of him that the '*dignity* (*semnotēs*) of Nicias was not of the harsh and offensive sort, but was blended with much circumspection' (Plutarch, *Nicias* 2). In this dignified gravity there was no arrogance; it was dignity and courtesy combined.

It is easy to see what a great quality this word *semnos* describes. It describes the divinity of the gods; it describes the Furies, the Erinyes who are the agents of divine justice; it describes the royalty of all true kingliness; it describes that which is stately and dignified in words and speech and conduct; it describes the characteristic of the man who carries himself with the perfect blend of dignity and courtesy, independence and humility to his fellow men.

R. C. Trench says that the man who is *semnos* 'has a grace and dignity not lent to him from earth, but which he owes to that higher citizenship which is also his'. The Latin word for this *dignity* is *gravitas*, and Tertullian writes: '*Ubi metus in Deum, ibi gravitas honesta,*' 'Where there is fear towards God, there is honourable dignity' (Tertullian, *De Praescriptione* 43.)

Clement of Alexandria summed it up when he said that a Christian man is *semnos* because his life is turned to the divine (Clement of Alexandria, *Stromateis* 7.35.6). This Christian kingliness and majesty and dignity come to a man when his face is turned to God, for then the reflection of God shines in him.

It is of the greatest significance that the Pastoral Epistles make so much of the majesty of the Christian life. They were written in the missionary days of the early Church. They were written when the Church was a little island of Christianity surrounded by a pagan world. At such a time it was not sermons but lives which won men for Christ. And men were won for Christ by the sight of the sheer majesty of the Christian life. So often the Christian life is beset by pettiness. So often the professing Christian allows little and petty things to disturb his own serenity and the peace of the brethren. We should do well to think of this essential majesty of the Christian life, and seek for more of it in our own lives.

There is a famous incident from the greatest days of Roman history. Pyrrhus had sent Kineas as his ambassador to Rome, and Kineas had been received by the Roman senate; he returned to Pyrrhus and told him that he had seen and talked with 'an assembly of kings'.

To him the Roman senate seemed nothing less than an assembly of kings. That is what the Christian Church should be like. The Christian should be *semnos*; he should ever display in his life the majesty of Christian living.

SOPHIA, PHRONĒSIS, SUNESIS

THE MIND EQUIPPED

T H E Greeks had three great words describing three great qualities of the mind; and if a man possessed these three qualities he had a mind equipped. The NT writers took over these three great words, for they were sure that the qualities which they describe were to be found in Jesus and in Jesus alone.

The first of these words is *sophia*. *Sophia* is generally translated *wisdom*; but the wisdom it describes is *the wisdom of ultimate things*. The Greek writings have many a great definition of *sophia*. The commonest definition is that *sophia* is 'the knowledge of things both human and divine and of their causes' (Clement of Alexandria, *Stromateis* 1.30.1).

Aristotle defined *sophia* as 'the most perfect of the modes of knowledge, not only of conclusions but also of first principles'. He said that *sophia* was 'consummated knowledge of the most exalted subjects' (Aristotle, *Nicomachean Ethics* 1141a 20).

Augustine said that *sophia* 'pertains to the knowledge of eternal things' (Augustine, *De Div. Quaest.* 2.2). Cicero said that *sophia*—which he translates *sapientia*—'is knowledge of things both human and divine' (Cicero, *Tusculan Disputations* 4.26) and he said that it was 'the chief of all the virtues' (Cicero, *De Officiis* 1.43). *Sophia* is that·ultimate knowledge which is nothing else than the knowledge of God. *Sophia* is the furthest reach of the human mind.

It is to be noted that, although *sophia* can be perverted into a bad thing, *sophia* itself is always noble and always implies goodness. Plato said: 'All *wisdom* (*sophia*) which is divorced from justice and the rest of virtue is craftiness and not wisdom' (Plato, *Menex.* 19). Xenophon quotes

Socrates as saying: 'Justice and every other form of virtue is *wisdom, sophia*' (Xenophon, *Memorabilia* 3.9.5). To the Greek *sophia, wisdom*, and goodness and nobility go hand in hand. The one cannot exist without the other.

The second of the three great words is *phronēsis*, which is usually translated *prudence*. The basic difference between *sophia* and *phronēsis* is that *sophia* is *theoretical*, and *phronēsis* is *practical; sophia* has to do with a man's mind and thought; *phronēsis* has to do with his life and conduct and action.

Aristotle defined *phronēsis* as 'truth . . . concerned with action in relation to the things that are good for human beings' (Aristotle, *Nicomachean Ethics* 1140b 20). He defined it as 'a virtue of mind by which men can come to wise decisions about the things which are called good and bad in relation to happiness' (Aristotle, *Rhetoric* 1366b 20).

Plutarch says that 'that virtue which considers what ought to be done and what ought not to be done is called *phronēsis*' (Plutarch, *De Virt. Mor.* 440 f.; he is really quoting a philosopher called Aristo). Plato defined it as 'that disposition of mind whereby we judge what is to be done and what is not to be done' (Plato *Definitions* 4.11).

Cicero defined *phronēsis*—he translates it by the word *prudentia*—as 'knowledge of what things are to be sought and what things are to be avoided'. Philo defined *phronēsis* as 'the correct mean between craftiness and folly' (Philo, *De Proem. et Poen.* 14).

Phronēsis is an extremely practical virtue. A writer in one of the papyri speaks of '*phronesis, prudence*, which increases a man's belongings'. There is a pessimistic papyrus poem which says: 'Whosoever thinks to prosper through *phronesis, prudence*, his hopes are vain. For all things in this life happen not through *phronēsis, prudence*, but through *tuchē, chance.*'

Very often the classical writers contrast and compare *sophia* and *phronēsis*. Philo says that *sophia* has got to do with the service of God; *phronēsis* has got to do with the arrangement of human life (*De Proem. et Poen.* 14).

Aristotle says that *sophia* has to do with the unchangeable things, whereas *phronēsis* has to do with changeable things, with what is expedient in any given set of circumstances (Aristotle, *Magn. Mor.* 1197a 34). Panaetius, the Stoic, said that *sophia* is the knowledge of things human and divine, but *phronēsis* is the knowledge of things good and evil and of things which are neither good nor evil (Diogenes Laertius, 7.92).

The third of the great Greek words of the mind is *sunesis*. *Sunesis* literally means a *uniting*, a *union*, a *bringing together*; and it would be true to say that *sunesis* is the *faculty of putting two and two together*. Aristotle said that *sunesis* was concerned only with judgment (Aristotle, *Nicomachean Ethics* 1143a 10). Demosthenes said that *sunesis* was a kind of conclusion, 'that by which fair and base things are distinguished'. When Thucydides is describing how the chances of war can be assessed he says that 'knowledge, *sunesis*, fortifies courage' (Thucydides, 2.62). That is, an intelligent assessment of the situation gives ground and strength to courage. When he is talking of a barbarian nation, he admits their courage and their strength, but, he says 'they are not on a level with other races in *general intelligence, sunesis*, and the arts of civilized life' (Thucydides, 2.97). They do not possess the developed faculty of judgment which civilized peoples possess. Aristotle says that children develop *sunesis*. 'Parents love their children as soon as they are born,' he says, 'but children only love their parents when time has elapsed and when they have acquired *understanding, sunesis*, or at least perception' (Aristotle, *Nicomachean Ethics* 1161b 26).

From all this we see that in its essence *sunesis* is critical. It is the power of distinguishing between different courses of action, different values of things, different relationships between people. *Sunesis* is the ability to test and to distinguish and to criticize and to evaluate and to form judgments.

So then we see that the mind equipped has three kinds of wisdom; it has the wisdom which can see and understand the ultimate and the infinite things; it has the wisdom which can deal with the practical problems of daily life and living; it has the wisdom which can judge and test things and choose the right aim and the right course of action in any actual situation.

It is interesting and important to note that over and over again the Bible joins together the theoretical wisdom which is in *sophia* and the practical wisdom which is in *phronēsis* and *sunesis*. On the Bible view of life a man needs both. Solomon prays that he may receive *wisdom, sophia,* and *understanding, phronēsis,* a wise and understanding heart (I Kings 3.12; 4.29). In the version of the same story in Chronicles, David prays that God may give Solomon *wisdom, sophia,* and *intelligence, sunesis,* and that is Solomon's prayer for himself (I Chron. 22.12; II Chron. 1.10). The four wise children in the Daniel story have knowledge and skill and learning and wisdom (Dan. 1.17). *Wisdom, sophia,* and *understanding, phronēsis,* both summon men to listen to them (Prov. 8.1). To keep God's commandments is the sign of *wisdom* and *understanding* (Deut. 4.6). Isaiah talks of the *wisdom* of the wise man, and the *understanding, sunesis,* of the prudent man (Isa. 29.14).

The great interest of this is that the really wise man has both theoretical and practical wisdom. Anatole France said of certain scholars that they have ink in their veins instead of blood and that they have never looked out of the window. It is quite true that the picture of the wise man is often the picture of a man locked in his study and buried in his books and lost in his research, a man quite out of touch with life, and indeed quite inefficient in the day-to-day conduct of life, the man who is epitomized in the absent-minded professor. Both the Greek and the biblical

view of life would say that such a man is an incomplete
man because though he may have *sophia* he certainly has
neither *phronēsis* nor *sunesis*. On the other hand, the common picture of the practical man is that he is so busy with
the practical concerns of life that he has neither the time
nor the inclination to trouble himself with theology or
philosophy or just plain thinking. Again that man is
incomplete because he may have *phronēsis* and *sunesis*,
but he has not got *sophia*.

The great vision of biblical thought is the vision of a
complete man who is wise in the things of eternity and
efficient in the things of time.

We must now turn to consider these words in the NT
itself, and with them we will consider their corresponding
adjectives. The adjective of *sophia*, wisdom, is *sophos*, wise.
The adjective of *phronēsis*, prudence, is *phronimos*, prudent.
The adjective of *sunesis*, understanding, is *sunetos*, understanding.

(i) Wisdom is the property of God (Rev. 5.12). Jesus
speaks of the wisdom of God (Luke 11.49); Paul also speaks
of the wisdom of God (Rom. 11.33), and the manifold
wisdom of God (Eph. 3.10). To know God is the only true
wisdom.

(ii) Wisdom is the characteristic of Jesus (Rev. 7.12).
Jesus grew in wisdom when he was a lad in Nazareth (Luke
2.40, 52). When he preached in Nazareth, the people asked
where he had acquired the wisdom which was so evident
in his words. (Matt. 13.54; cp. Mark 6.2.) He himself is
wisdom, the wisdom of God (I Cor. 1.24, 30). In him are
all the treasures of wisdom (Col. 2.3). Jesus is wisdom
because he came to bring us the knowledge of God, which
is the only wisdom which matters.

(iii) Wisdom is the distinguishing feature of the men
who were great. Solomon had wisdom (Matt. 12.42; cp.
Luke 11.31). Joseph had wisdom which kept him in the
right way and raised him to greatness in Egypt (Acts 7.10).
Moses was trained in wisdom (Acts 7.22). The qualifications

of the first office-bearers in the Church, the Seven, were that they must be men full of the Holy Ghost and of wisdom (Acts 6.3). Stephen had a wisdom with which he confounded the Jews in his debates with them (Acts 6.10). The prophets and the wise men are classed together (Matt. 23.34). It is when a man knows God that he is really wise.

(iv) Wisdom is the mark of the Christian. It was the promise of Jesus that he would give his followers wisdom with which they could confront their enemies and their persecutors (Luke 21.15). It is Paul's prayer that God would give his people wisdom and prudence (Eph. 1.8), that God would give them the spirit of wisdom (Eph. 1.17). Wisdom is the object of Paul's prayers and of his teaching (Col. 1.9; 1.28). The Christian walks in wisdom (Col. 4.5). The man who produces works to fit his faith is the man of wisdom (James 3.13). The Christian has that wisdom which gives him an answer to his opponents and a solution to his problems. The Christian is wise unto that which is good (Rom. 16.19).

(v) Wisdom is connected with prayer and with the Holy Spirit and with God. The Seven were to be men filled with the Holy Spirit and with wisdom (Acts 6.3). God gives it to the man who lacks it (James 1.5). The real wisdom is heavenly (James 3.15). And we have already seen that Paul prays that wisdom should be given to God's people (Eph. 1.17; Col. 1.9). The word of wisdom in preaching is the gift of the Spirit (I Cor. 12.8). The only wisdom which matters is not man's discovery; it is God's gift.

(vi) And yet, though that be so, wisdom can be taught, for it is Paul's endeavour to teach it (Col. 1.28). There is a development in wisdom, for Paul speaks wisdom among the mature Christians (I Cor. 2.6, 7). There is clearly growth in wisdom. Although wisdom is not the discovery of the mind, it cannot be obtained without the strenuous activity of the mind. Real wisdom comes when the Spirit of God reaches down to meet the searching mind of man, but the mind of man must search before God will come to meet it. Wisdom is not for the mentally lazy even although it is the gift of God.

(vii) Wisdom reads the true meaning of things (Rev. 13.18; 17.9). God's messages are there for the man who has eyes to see and mind to understand. In this it is blessedly true that the man who seeks will find.

But great as wisdom is, it can degenerate. Especially in I Corinthians Paul has a great deal to say about the wrong kind of wisdom.

(i) The degenerate wisdom is worldly wisdom, wisdom of this world (I Cor. 1.20; 2.6; 1.26; 3.18). It is the kind of wisdom which knows well how to get on in this world and how to amass the treasures of this world, but has no knowledge of the things that matter.

(ii) It is a wisdom of words. It is a wisdom of words which in the end do nothing but obscure the Cross (I Cor. 1.17). Paul refuses to preach with the enticing words of man's wisdom (I Cor. 2.1, 4, 5, 13). When Paul so strongly condemned the worldly wisdom of words, he was speaking out of the situation of the world of his day. The Greeks had always loved words; and one of the well-known figures of the Greek world was the Sophist. The Sophist was the orator who was as famous as a film star. The Sophist had two faults. He was much more concerned with how he said a thing than with what he was saying. It was cleverness of speech with which he was primarily concerned; and his first aim was to provoke applause. His one desire was to display himself. Dio Chrysostom said of the Sophists: 'They are all agape for the murmur of the crowd. . . . Like men walking in the dark, they move always in the direction of the clapping and the shouting.' (Dio Chrysostom, *Oration* 33.) One of them said to Epictetus: 'I want your praise.' 'What do you mean by my praise?' asked Epictetus. 'I want you to say Bravo! and Wonderful!' said the Sophist (Epictetus, *Discourses* 3.23.24). Epictetus describes the scene as the professor went round after the lecture was done. 'What did you think of me to-day?' 'Upon my life I thought you were admirable.' 'What did you think of my best passage?' 'Which was that?' 'Where I described Pan and the Nymphs.' 'Oh, it was excessively well done' (Epictetus, *Discourses* 3.23.11). He describes another scene. 'A much larger audience to-day, I think,' says the professor. 'Yes, much larger.' 'Five hundred, I should guess.' 'Oh, nonsense, it could not have been less than a thousand.' 'Why, that is more than Dio ever had; I wonder why it was: they appreciated what I said, too.' 'Beauty, sir, can move even a stone.'

Paul knew the preachers and the teachers who were more concerned with epigrams than truth, whose one desire was to display their own cleverness and to awaken the applause of the crowd. He knew the preacher and the teacher who was thinking more of what men were thinking of him than what God was thinking of him.

He knew the preacher and the teacher who was more concerned that men should look at him than that men should look at Christ. That is what Paul meant by the wisdom of this world. It is not yet completely dead.

(iii) Such wisdom did not really know God (I Cor. 1.21). It was seductive far more than it was instructive (I Cor. 2.4, 5). It was man's wisdom, not God's wisdom (I Cor. 2.13). It was the wisdom of the clever debater who was more concerned with a display of mental acrobatics than with the search for the truth (I Cor. 1.20). It was vain in the sense that it helped nobody and achieved nothing (I Cor. 3.20). In the end it was doomed to destruction and to the condemnation of God and to the demonstration of the folly which it in reality was (I Cor. 1.19; 1.27; 3.19).

The only true wisdom is the outcome, not of pride, but of humility. The only wise teaching points not at itself, but beyond itself. Wisdom ceases when a man's sole desire is to be clever. Preaching degenerates whenever it seeks for applause. Whenever the personality and methods of the teacher and the preacher obscure Christ then there is no wisdom in it, and it degenerates into the foolishness which in the end will receive the conviction and the condemnation it deserves.

Now let us look at the companion words, *phronēsis* and *phronimos, sunesis* and *sunetos*.

Phronēsis, the noun, only occurs twice in the NT, in Luke 1.17 and Eph. 1.8. But *phronimos*, its corresponding adjective, occurs more frequently. *Phronēsis*, as we saw, is the practical wisdom which sees what must be done and what must not be done in any given situation. The builder who built his house on a rock was *phronimos* (Matt. 7.24). The disciple in face of the world must be *phronimos* as a serpent (Matt. 10.16). The wise steward who orders the household well is *phronimos* (Matt. 24.45; cp. Luke 12.42). The virgins who remembered the oil for their lamps are *phronimos* (Matt. 25.2, 4, 8, 9). When Paul is addressing the Corinthians, he says in appeal to their common sense: ' I speak as to wise men' (*phronimoi*) (I Cor. 10.15).

This practical wisdom can on occasion degenerate into conceit (Rom. 11.25; 12.16; I Cor. 4.10; II Cor. 11.19). A man can become too impressed with his own cleverness. In Barrie's novel, *Sentimental Tommy*, when Tommy had done something clever at school, he used to come home and say to Elspeth, his admiring sister: ' Am I no' a wonder? ' This practical wisdom can be like that.

There are two passages which specially show the meaning of *phronimos*. The serpent who seduced Adam and Eve in the garden is called *phronimos* (Gen. 3.1); and the unjust steward who first swindled his master and then took steps to safeguard his own ease and comfort is called *phronimos* (Luke 16.8). *Phronēsis* is above all the ability to deal with a given situation; it is the ability to see what needs to be done and to do it; it is the practical wisdom of the man who is never at a loss.

Sunesis and *sunetos* are not very frequent in the NT. The scribe answered Jesus that men are to love God with all their hearts, and *understanding, sunesis*, and soul and strength. The Jewish Rabbis were amazed at Jesus' *sunesis* when he was with them in the Temple Court (Luke 2.47). Sergius Paulus, the Roman governor, is described as *sunetos* (Acts 13.7). In Eph. 3.4 *sunesis* describes Paul's understanding of God's secret. In Col. 1.9 Paul prays that his people may have *sophia* and *sunesis*; and in Col. 2.2 *sunesis* can bring assurance. It is Paul's prayer for the young Timothy that God will give him understanding, *sunesis*, in all things (II Tim. 2.7). It too can be a worldly and conceited thing and when it does become so it will be destroyed (I Cor. 1.19). Jesus says that the great things are hidden from the wise and the prudent (*sophoi* and *sunetoi*) and revealed to babes (Matt. 11.25; cp. Luke 10.21).

The essence of *sunesis* is the critical faculty which, as Lightfoot puts it 'sees the bearing of things'. Its essence is discrimination and wise judgment. It can see the implications of a thing and the ultimate end of a course of action. It sees a thing, not only as it is at the moment, but as it will be.

The Christian equipment of the mind is a many-sided thing. There is the wisdom, *sophia*, which sees the ultimate truths of God, there is the practical wisdom, *phronēsis*, which sees what ought to be done in any given situation; there is the discriminating, critical wisdom, *sunesis*, which can assess and evaluate every course of action which presents itself. The Christian is not only the dreamer whose thoughts are long, long thoughts and who is detached from this world; the Christian is not only the man of affairs who never thinks of ultimate things; the Christian is not only the shrewd evaluator of any policy or any situation. The Christian is all three. He has not only the vision to know God; he has the practical knowledge to turn that vision into action, and the sound judgment to see what course of action will best achieve his aim. The Christian is the only man who is dreamer and man of action at one and the same time.

SPLAGCHNIZESTHAI

THE DIVINE COMPASSION

T H E R E are some words which bear within themselves the
evidence of a kind of revolution in the realm of thought:
and *splagchnizesthai* is such a word. It means *to be moved
with compassion*. It is not a classical word, but it does
contain a classical way of thought. *Splagchnizesthai* is the
verb which comes from the noun *splagchna*, which means
what are known as the nobler viscera, that is, the heart, the
lungs, the liver and the intestines. The Greeks held these to
be the seat of the emotions, especially of anger, of anxiety,
of fear, and even of love. When Hercules is expressing his
complaint to Admetus, he says: 'Unto a friend behoveth
speech outspoken, Admetus, not to hide within the *splagchna* (the breast, as we would say in English) murmurs
unvoiced' (Euripides, *Alcestis* 1008-1010). When the Chorus
are listening to Electra's lamentation, they say: 'My
splagchna are overcast with gloom at thy speech' (Aeschylus, *Choephori* 413). So then in classical Greek the *splagchna*
mean the inner parts of man, which are the seat of the
deepest emotions. It is from that idea that the verb *splagchnizesthai* was formed in later Greek. It means *to be
moved with compassion*, and, from its very derivation, it
can be seen that it describes no ordinary pity or compassion, but an emotion which moves a man to the very depths
of his being. It is the strongest word in Greek for the feeling
of compassion.

In the NT the word never occurs outside the Synoptic
Gospels; and except for three occurrences in the parables
it is always used of Jesus. In the parables it is used of the
master who had *compassion* on the servant who was un-
able to pay his debt (Matt. 18.33); of the *compassion* which
made the father welcome home the prodigal son (Luke

15.20); and of the *compassion* which made the Samaritan go to the help of the wounded traveller on the Jericho road (Luke 10.33). In all other cases it is used of Jesus himself.

Jesus was *moved with compassion* when he saw the crowd like sheep without a shepherd (Matt. 9.36; cp. Mark 6.34). He was *moved with compassion* when he saw their hunger and their need when they had followed him out to the desert place (Matt. 14.14; 15.32; Mark 8.2). It is used of Jesus' *compassion* on the leper (Mark 1.41; it is possible that another reading should be preferred in this passage); of his *compassion* on the two blind men (Matt. 20.34); of his *compassion* on the widow at Nain who was going to bury her only son (Luke 7.13); and the appeal of the man with the epileptic son is that Jesus should have *compassion* on him (Mark 9.22).

There are two interesting things about the use of this word. First, it shows us the things in the human situation which moved the heart of Jesus.

(i) Jesus was moved by the *spiritual lostness of the crowd*. They were as sheep without a shepherd. He was not annoyed with their foolishness, he was not angry at their shiftlessness; he was sorry for them. He saw them as a harvest waiting to be gathered for God (Matt. 9.37, 38). The Pharisees said: 'The man who does not know the law is accursed.' They were able to say: 'There is joy in heaven over one sinner who is destroyed.' But in face of man's lostness, even when that lostness was his own fault, Jesus felt nothing but pity. He did not see man as a criminal to be condemned; he saw man as a lost wanderer to be found and brought home. He did not see men as chaff to be burned; he saw them as a harvest to be reaped for God.

(ii) Jesus was moved by the *hunger and the pain of men*. The sight of a crowd of hungry, tired people, the appeal of a blind or a leprous man, moved him to compassion. He never regarded people as a nuisance, but always as people whom he must help. Eusebius (*Ecclesiastical History* 10.4.11) writes of Jesus in words which are either an unconscious or a deliberate quotation from Hippocrates, the founder of Greek medicine. 'He was like some excellent physician, who, in order to cure the sick, examines what is repulsive, handles sores, and reaps pain himself from the sufferings of others.' Jesus never regarded the sufferer with indifference, still less with loathing and disgust. He regarded the sufferer and the needy with a pity which issued in help.

(iii) Jesus was moved by the *sorrow of others*. When he met the funeral procession of the son of the widow of Nain, he was moved by the pathos of the human situation. He was not detached and he was not indifferent; the sorrow of the widow was his own sorrow. In *Sentimental Tommy* Barrie wrote of his hero, who is himself : 'The most conspicuous of his traits was the faculty of stepping into other people's shoes and remaining in them until he became someone else.' The greatness of Jesus was his willingness to enter into the human situation, and to be moved by its poignancy to that compassion which compelled him to help and to heal.

But this word *splagchnizesthai* has a far greater significance than simply the indication that Jesus was moved to the depths of his being by the human situation. The notable thing about this word is that to a Greek its use about anyone who was divine would seem completely and utterly and totally incredible.

According to the Stoics, and they were the highest thinkers of the age, the supreme and essential characteristic of God is *apatheia*. By *apatheia* they did not mean *apathy*, in the sense of indifference. They meant *incapability of feeling*. They argued in this way. If a man can feel either sorrow or joy, it means that someone else can bring sorrow or joy to him. That is to say, it means that someone else can affect him. Now, if someone else can affect him, can alter his feelings, can make him happy or sad, it means that that person has power over him, and is therefore, for the moment at least, greater than he. If God could feel sorrow or joy at anything that happens to man, it would mean that man can affect God, that man has that much power over God; but it is impossible that anyone should have any power over God, for no one can be greater than God; therefore God can have no feeling, he must be essentially without feeling; he must be, in the technical sense of the word, by nature *apathetic*. The Greeks believed in a God who could not feel. To them a divine being who was moved with compassion was incredible.

When Apuleius was writing about the god of Socrates, he said that, according to Plato's thought, 'never God and man can meet. A stone will hear me more easily than Jupiter.' He goes on to say that he does not think so much that the gods are separate and different from us, but that it is quite impossible that our prayers should reach them. 'Not from the care of human affairs, but from contact have I removed them' (*De Deo Socr.* 6.132). If God is God, then he is such that he is essentially incapable of hearing any prayer, or feeling any pity.

When Plutarch was thinking about God, he held that God was quite above having any contact whatsoever with the universe. Any contact of the universe with the divine came through intermediaries, who were the daemons. He said : ' He who involves God in human needs, does not spare his majesty, nor does he maintain the dignity and greatness of God's excellence' (Plutarch, *De Def. Orac.* 9, 414 f). As Plutarch saw it, it was impossible for God to be God and to be in the least involved in or affected by human affairs. Once again, to such a thinker it would be beyond belief that God could be moved with compassion.

But the Christian point of view stresses this very pity of God. God, said Clement of Alexandria, is 'rich in pity'. God is indeed—it is a wonderful picture—all ear and all eye (Clement of Alexandria, *Stromateis* 2.74.4; 7.37.6). He says of the Logos, the Word of God, that though he was essentially and eternally free from passion, 'for our sake he took upon himself our flesh with its capacity for suffering' and 'descended to sensation' (*Stromateis* 5.40.3). To Clement the very essence of the Christian idea of God was that God voluntarily choose to feel for and with men.

The grim thing about pagan ethics was that the Stoics taught that man should seek to make himself like God, and not to care. If a man wanted peace, they argued, he should banish all feeling, all emotion from his mind. Epictetus writes of how we should teach and train ourselves not to care when we lose something. 'This should be our study from morning to night, beginning from the least and frailest things, from an earthen vessel, from a glass. Afterwards, proceed to a suit of clothes, a dog, a horse, an estate; from thence to your self, body, parts of the body, children, wife, brothers' (Epictetus, *Discourses* 4.1. 13). Lose anything, see your nearest and dearest die, and say: 'It doesn't matter; I don't care.'

Pagan religious thought believed in a God whose essence was that he was incapable of feeling pity; pagan ethics taught that the aim of life was a life from which all pity and all compassion were totally and finally banished. The idea of a God who could be moved with compassion, and of a life whose motive force was pitying love, must have come to such a world literally like a new revelation.

We think it a commonplace that God is love, and that the Christian life is love. We would do well to remember that we would never have known that without the revelation of Jesus Christ, of whom it is so often and so amazingly said that he was moved with compassion.